Joe

The Horse Nobody Loved

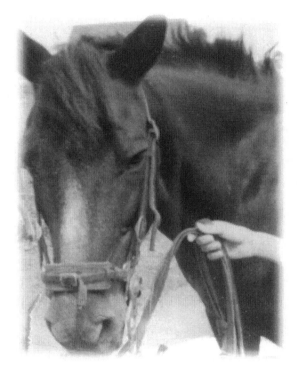

Vicky Kaseorg

Vicky Kaseorg

Edited by Alex McGilvery

Cover design by Gina Keesling of Hoofprints.com

Copyright 2015

All rights reserved by author

ISBN 13: 978-1511515726

*Author's Note

The horse in this story is a real horse from my childhood. The major events as depicted are all true. However, all the characters outside of my own family names have been changed and many of them are conglomerates of people I knew at the time. It is important to note that this story occurred fifty years ago, and is told through the eyes of the child I was at the time. It is not intended to be an objective portrayal, but one filtered through the eyes of a nine-year-old lonely little girl. The town is a fictitious town, but the descriptions all match the actual place where the story transpired as I remembered it a half century later.

Joe 1968

Vicky Kaseorg

Chapter One

Funny, I can't remember what I had for lunch, but I remember Joe the horse a half century later with exquisite detail. I can still picture his muzzle with the tufts of stiff hair poking out, his potbelly, his deeply swayed back, his gentle brown eyes. The picture of that horse is indelibly etched into my memory as though it were my own hand I was gazing at. Joe is a part of me, I guess. Joe was critical in molding the person I became. But back then, I just thought Joe was a horse that nobody loved….except for me.

I was nine-years-old when we moved from Tennessee to Illinois. A painfully shy child, I wet my pants in third grade rather than dare raise my hand to ask the teacher if I could go to the bathroom. Another terrible humiliation occurred in first grade in Memphis. The teacher paddled me in front of the class because I didn't turn my head away from the window during naptime. (This was in the good old days when teachers had the right to wallop miscreants in their classrooms.) One moment, I was contentedly gazing out the window, day-dreaming about the sun, the sky, and the shapes the clouds made. Next thing I know, the teacher hauled me to the front of the room as an example to dissuade children from following the certain life of reprobates and felons that my delinquent behavior foretold. Maybe that experience is what shaped me to homeschool my own children one day rather than subject them to public school.

Anyway, I don't think I was very sorrowful at age nine to leave Memphis behind, particularly when I discovered that there was a horse farm a mile from our new house in the Chicago suburb of Chazak. We lived on Narroway Rd. which is a major bustling busy highway now. Fifty years ago, it was a two-lane highway and I knew not to go near it, but Chazak itself was nothing like what it is now.

I was horse crazy. I was a very good artist, and when I wasn't reading about horses, I was drawing them. You cannot imagine my delight when I discovered that horse farm! On the other hand, had my parents closely examined Burton's Farm before letting me head off on my own to visit it, they might have experienced a slightly different emotion…like horror.

My Mom practiced a form of parenting she calls *Benign Neglect.* Many of the parents of the 50's and 60's practiced this type of child-rearing. Basically, she shooed us out the door shortly after sunrise in the morning, and sometimes even locked it. We were expected to stay alive as well as possible, and she would unlock the door for meals. I thought she was a very good mother, and I loved the freedom. If we were in danger of dying, (which frankly we often were,) we lucked out, because I can't think of a single one of us who suffered from this system.

Understanding this background casts light on why I walked a mile to the farm, alongside such a busy highway, all by myself, at age nine. I planned to muster every molecule of bravery from my pathetically timid soul and ask the horse farm owner for a job.

Now, even naïve as I was, I knew it was unlikely they would pay money to hire a nine-year-old girl. I also knew not the slightest thing about horses, except that I loved them and would do anything to be around them. So that was my plan. I would offer to do *anything*, in exchange for being near the horses. Let the chips fall where they may.

I headed out to the farm. I don't even know if my mother knew where I was going. She may have, but in all likelihood, she did not. She wouldn't miss me till dinner time. As I approached the farm, crossing the last street of the neighborhood, the glorious farm opened up like a vision before me. Now mind you, to most people, that glorious vision was a falling down, decrepit barn, barbed wire fences with rusty posts surrounding several fields without a single blade of grass, knee-deep mud, and some dusty trails that lined the edge of the pastures. The horses were a motley collection, one neigh away from a dog-food can. Rusty cars and broken machinery dotted the area in front of the barn. A vicious Doberman was tied to the edge of a shed, and when anyone came near, he leaped to his feet, straining at his barbed collar and baring teeth as sharp as razors and as long as swords. Nonetheless, except for the scary dog, in my eyes it was a vision of heaven.

As I rounded the corner into the main entrance, the dog went bananas.

"Shut up, Zeke!" a deep voice bellowed, which had zero effect on the dog.

From inside the shed came a frenzied whinnying and the sound of a large creature kicking violently at the already fragile looking walls. I later learned that was the stallion of the farm. He was as mean as the dog, and even more dangerous since he had about 2,000 pounds on Zeke. Zeke however could climb ladders, especially when there were tasty little girls cowering in the hayloft (don't ask me how I know that…) The stallion couldn't do *that*, but he could easily have kicked the supports down that held the hayloft up.

I took a deep breath, and hurried towards the opening of the ramshackle barn. The man who had bellowed at the dog sat on a pile of hay bales, watching me approach. He was chewing on a piece of straw. Next to him stood a grizzled, tough looking woman with skin like sandpaper. She was the most weathered human being I had ever seen. I figured she must be at least one hundred-years-old. Both she and the man wore ragged clothes that were filthy and torn.

Even if I hadn't been an abnormally shy child, the sight of those two would have given me the runs. But anyone who knows me knows that I have determination the size of a small planet. I was on a mission, and fear, even mind-numbing fear, was not going to deter me.

"Hello," the woman said.

I was surprised by her smile, and the kindness in her voice. It didn't match her exterior at all. Her eyes crinkled and a million wrinkles shot out from the edge of them like cracks in the ice.

"I'm Vicky, and I would like to volunteer. I'll do anything you want me to do if I can just be around the horses." Whew. I almost passed out with the monumental effort of that sentence, but it was said and done. I'd said my piece I'd practiced the whole mile walking along Narroway Road. Now, it was up to God, and that scary couple.

The woman continued to smile, and the man laughed. I turned beet red, and bit my lip to keep from crying.

"Well," he said, "That is quite some speech for such a skinny little thing."

"Burton," admonished the woman, "Leave her be. So, Vicky, do you live near here?"

I nodded.

"Did you walk here?"

I nodded again.

"Cat got your tongue?" Burton asked.

I nodded.

The woman glared at him and then turned back to me.

"Have you ever worked around horses before?"

I shook my head.

"Well what makes you think you want to volunteer here then?" she asked.

"Milly, weren't you listening? She wants to be around them."

I peeked at Burton through my downcast eyes. He was grinning at me, and not in an unfriendly way.

"I love horses," I squeaked, "And I am a hard worker. I can help you clean the stalls."

"That's smelly, hard work," Milly said, "You would do that, just to be near horses?"

I nodded.

"Let me show you a stall," she said. She stood up, and I followed her down a dark hallway just inside the barn. She swung open a stall door and waved her hand at the contents of the enclosure. The stench almost knocked me out. This is no exaggeration. The manure was at least a foot deep. Maybe more. Layers of soggy straw were wedged between putrid heavy sandwiches of excrement. If I'd ever seen anything more disgusting in my life, I can't recall it.

"What do you think?" she asked, her eyes twinkling, "Would you clean *that* just to be near a horse?"

I peered into the stall, trying not to breathe through my nose. Turning back to Milly, I nodded.

She lifted an eyebrow, and glanced at Burton.

"When do you want to start?" he asked.

"Now," I said firmly. I had to, or I might never get up the nerve again.

Milly shook her head, a grin spreading across her face. I watched more wrinkles span out and was really worried pieces of her face would dislodge and crash to the ground. She shrugged her shoulders at Burton and walked back into the main barn. She snatched a pitchfork from a hook on the wall, and returned to the stall.

"OK, Vicky. Have you ever used a pitchfork?"

I shook my head, still trying not to breathe through my nose, but worried that I might suck one of the few thousand flies that darted about into my mouth. So I parted my lips but kept my teeth clenched like a jail cell. I can't imagine I looked like a normal child.

"You hold it like this, and you'll get under the top layer of muck, like this…"

She demonstrated. As soon as she hefted a piece of the layered miasma onto the pitchfork, steam rose and with it, an impossibly more toxic smell than before. Milly seemed incredibly impervious to the aroma that almost toppled me.

"Now, let me get you a wheelbarrow. What you'll do is load the wheelbarrow, and then when it is about half way full, you wheel it over to that pile across the yard.

'Yard' is the word they used for the stretch of dirt and gravel just outside the main barn. There was not one blade of grass, though there were some thistley weeds, with prickers on them. On the opposite side of the yard was a series of small sheds and tottering buildings. Chickens hopped nearby. On the other side of the building was a fenced enclosure with several goats inside. The pile Milly pointed to with the pitchfork was a towering mass of manure.

"Don't fill the wheelbarrow very high at first," she warned, "It is very heavy and you are probably not used to how hard it will be to push it."

I nodded. She handed me the pitchfork.

"Ready to try?"

I took the pitchfork, and she stepped back. I stabbed it deep into the manure mass. Then I heaved, and huffed, and puffed, but there was no way I was going to lift that heavy forkful.

"Don't stab so deeply," she said, "You have to skim a little at a time off the top."

Well, that made sense. I tried again. This time I managed to lift a much smaller section, but it was still incredibly heavy, and the smell....oh my. The smell was so concentrated, I was afraid it would explode. I wasn't positive that could happen, but if bad smells were dynamite, this stall was an atom bomb. Even breathing through parted lips with clenched teeth did nothing to stop the dizzying nausea that washed over me. I struggled even with the small forkful, but somehow, I wrenched it over to the wheelbarrow and plopped it in.

"Nice job," Milly said, "When you get tired, come rest and I'll get you a bottle of pop."

She returned to Burton, and I was left alone with my work. I don't remember much of that first day cleaning the stall, except feeling very tired within minutes, but I was determined. Blisters quickly formed in between my thumb and first finger and along my palms. They hurt terribly, but I knew that if I quit too soon, they would know I was not up to the job. So as the blisters popped, and sweat poured off me, and flies bit my ankles, I shoveled the manure. When the wheelbarrow was half full, like Milly had advised, I set the pitchfork against the stall wall, and grabbed the splintery handles of the rickety wheelbarrow. I heaved. It didn't move an inch. Putting my full weight into shoving, it rolled ever so slightly forward. By now, I was straining to my utmost, and that wheelbarrow was going nowhere. Burton and Milly still sat on the hay bale, chatting, and oblivious to my predicament. I let go, backed up ten feet and then went racing at the wheelbarrow with a running start. Snatching the handles, I heaved. Miraculously, the momentum carried it forward and with my feet churning furiously, I managed to get the dangerously teetering wheelbarrow to move five feet.

At this point, Milly leaped up and came to my rescue. She grabbed it just as it was about to dump my half-hour of work on the (relatively) clean barn floor.

"Probably a tad too full for you," she said gently, "I'll dump this load." She pushed the wheelbarrow as though it were a kite on a string sailing across the sky. Sinewy muscles bulged on her arms. I watched in wonderment.

When she returned, she said, "That was a big load. You are a very good worker. Do you want to quit now?"

I did, of course, but I shook my head.

"I'm not tired," I said, lying through my clenched teeth. Burton and Milly exchanged a glance.

Milly rolled the wheelbarrow back in front of the stall, and I went back to work. I filled the wheelbarrow half as full as before. It was still very heavy, and it tottered unsteadily in my unfamiliar steerage, but I managed to get it safely to the pile.

I worked all day. Dinner time was the cue for Mom to count her progeny, so my inner clock kept track of that event drawing near. No need to wear a watch. I just had a sixth sense, like all kids did back then, about when I needed to head home. I didn't finish the stall, but had cleared at least half of it to the floor by the time I could do no more.

Milly came over as the shadows stretched across the yard. She looked at the stall.

"I don't think I've seen that floor in a year," she said.

I smiled. She crossed her arms and looked at me.

"Ok, Vicky. You got yourself a deal. And for your work for us, you get more than just looking at the horses. How would you like to learn to *ride* a horse?"

I stared at her, feeling like my heart would burst. And not just from the afternoon's exertion. I couldn't even nod, struck by unspeakable joy into physical and mental muteness.

"Unless you don't want to," she added.

"Oh no!" I said quickly, "I mean, oh yes! Yes, please, and thank you. I would like very much to learn how to ride!"

At that moment a lanky boy walked by. He was the spitting image of Burton, and I knew he must be the son. He was probably two or three years older than me. Dirty blond hair framed an impish face with a wicked grin. Mayhem and mishap sparkled from his steely blue eyes. I knew he was trouble from the moment I saw him. I also knew I was in love.

"Pee yew!!!" he said, holding his nose, as he passed me, "You smell like %%$$#^!"

"Mick!" Milly snapped, in rebuke.

"Well she does," Mick said.

He sauntered away, and I waited for Milly to smack him, or tell him to come back this minute and apologize. She did neither. She gazed after him with a look of adoration. I understood. I felt the same way.

She broke the reverential silence.

"If you feel up to it, I'd love for you to come back tomorrow," she said.

"I have school, but I'll come right after school," I promised.

I glanced at the sun low in the sky, and the shadows tiptoeing across the yard, nearly kicking the huge pile of manure.

"But I need to get going now," I said.

Milly nodded.

I waved awkwardly. Burton was gone as I walked out the front door by the hay bales. Zeke went ballistic again as I rounded the corner near his shed. I broke into a jog and headed alongside Narroway Rd., thinking I had never been so happy in my entire life.

CHAPTER TWO

I could barely stand it, plodding my way through school. I'd always been a good student, and even liked school, once I escaped enforced nap-times and the corporal punishment of Memphis. Nonetheless, I had a whole *universe* of difficulty trying to concentrate when the beautiful farm lurked in my every thought. My hands, with their raw blisters, were covered in bandages, which fell off every time I washed my hands. My muscles shrieked in pain from all that unfamiliar work of the day before. Still, I couldn't wait. *Oh when will this interminable day end?* Yes, I did use the word 'interminable.' Mom and Dad were forever using words longer than the day, and then asked us to look it up if we appeared confused.

"This is how you grow into the language," they told me.

Finally, the school bell rang, and we were released. A thousand-hour bus ride home while I jiggled in my seat. I ran all the way from the bus stop to our house, leaving my three siblings in the dust. Pausing at home only long enough to throw on some old clothes and the same (stinky) jacket I had worn the day before, I dashed out the door and jogged along Narroway Rd. I passed a skinny girl with buck teeth walking along the edge of the farm pasture. She glanced at me, and I raised a hand to wave. She turned her head, ignoring me.

As I rounded the corner, Zeke went ballistic, the stallion neighed and kicked a few walls with resounding thumps, and I skidded to a stop in front of the hay bales.

A tiny little girl, no bigger than a garden gnome, sat atop the bales where Burton had been the day before.

"Who the $$#@@%* are you?" she asked.

I blinked, frankly shocked to hear that kind of language out of someone so tiny. She could not have been more than five-years-old.

"Peeper, watch your mouth!" Milly said, emerging from the dark recesses of the barn, "Or I will kick the *$#@@%^* out of you."

Peeper pursed her lips.

"Who the heck are you?" she amended her first question.

"I'm Vicky," I said.

"The girl who smells like…" a deeper voice added.

"Mick!" Milly warned.

The devilish Mick had materialized from a back aisle of the barn, and hefted a bale of hay. He tossed it down and pulled off the strings. The hay bale fell open into rectangular pieces.

"Vicky," Milly said, "I am surprised you're back! I thought after all that work, you would be too sore to get out of bed."

I smiled at her, and nodded.

"But I am glad you are here," she said kindly, "And I have a job for you that will be easier today. Mick can show you how to feed the horses. He can teach you how much hay the inside stalls get, and then you can help throw some bales in the pasture."

Mick stared at his mother, pausing mid-bend as he scooped three rectangles of hay in his arms.

"I have to teach this little ###@%%^&* ? She's your project. Why don't you..."

With a roar, Burton appeared and backhanded Mick across the face. Mick wheeled from the smack, and a look of hatred crossed his face.

"Listen to your mother, and you be nice to Vicky."

Mick glared at me. I stood there with wide eyes, afraid to breathe.

"Why does your hair stick out like that?" Peeper asked, smiling at me.

I grabbed at my head and smoothed down the wayward frizz.

Mick laughed, glancing quickly at the retreating back of his father. "Cause it's made of hay. Leastwise, looks like it is," he whispered.

My cheeks burned, but I didn't speak. I could never think of a single thing to say until I was walking home from the situation, and then a thousand retorts tumbled like Olympic gymnasts across my mind.

"At least the hay-bales aren't *inside* my head, instead of *brains*, like yours," I said...not then, of course. But on my walk home I did. To his face, I said nothing.

I know Milly heard him, but she didn't say anything. I don't know how he could have hated me so intensely so quickly. Usually it takes folks time to get to know me before they hate me. Then he grinned, with that intoxicatingly adorable, devilish half grin.

"Can you count to four? That's how many sections of hay this line of stalls gets." He waited, looking expectantly at me.

"Do you need help? Peeper, count to four for hay-head."

"One, two, three, four…I can go higher," she said happily.

"That's too much for *her* to learn in one day," he said, nodding in my direction.

"Enough Mick," Milly growled from the back of the barn where she was opening a container of grain.

I stood mutely, ineffectually grasping about inside my brain for words.

Mick shook his head, as though he could not believe what an imbecile I was, and picked up his four sections and headed to the first stall. He tossed the hay over the door. That was the stall I had been cleaning yesterday. I was shocked that a horse was in there, standing ankle deep in that disgusting mess. And now his food was tossed in on top of all that rankness. I felt sorry for the horse. Were all horse farms this…filthy? I grabbed four sections and headed to the second stall. A black horse stuck his head over the door and gazed at me as I carefully dropped the hay at his feet. For a moment our eyes met. He had deep brown, gentle eyes. We stared kindly at each other, and then he dropped his head out of sight, and I heard him munching.

Mick seemed to have forgotten I was there as we passed each other back and forth on our treks gathering the hay and tossing it into the stalls.

These were the box stalls, I learned, and these horses were relatively prized. They belonged to the "rich boarders." Along another narrow corridor on the other side of the wide open central area of the barn was a row of standing stalls. Those were the "less rich boarders" horses. Mick called them something else I can't repeat or my mom would wash my mouth out with soap. *Most* of what Mick said would meet that fate in my house.

The narrow aisle was hedged by a wall on the right, and stalls lined the left side, with the mangers nearest the aisle. The horses' heads were tied to the front of the stall near the manger. We dropped the hay into the mangers. This part of the job was pure joy. I reached out and stroked several of the horse's foreheads. Mick never reached out to touch a single horse. He did his work silently, with a look of disdain. He saw me reach for one horse to pet the silky muzzle.

"That one bites."

I snatched my hand back. The horse gazed at me, munching his hay, and didn't look at all like he wanted to bite anything but his dinner.

"Douche-bag," said Mick, under his breath.

I heard a deep rumble from the yard, and followed Mick out of the barn. Burton sat atop a rusty red tractor, with a small flatbed trailer attached behind it. He hopped off the tractor, which continued to idle with spits and starts, and he scurried like a monkey up the vertical wooden ladder built as part of the barn wall. Without a word, he began tossing down hay bales. Mick gathered them one by one, and flung them onto the flatbed. With a grunt, he pointed his chin at the bales, and then nodded at the flatbed. Understanding, I hefted a bale. It was heavier than it looked, but I man-handled it to the flatbed, and with some difficulty, heaved it onto the old wood surface. We piled some twenty bales onto the trailer, and then Mick signaled to me from atop the truck bed.

"Come on."

I clambered onto the flatbed, and Burton reappeared after leaping the last ten feet from the ladder to the ground. He pinched Milly's bottom as he walked by her, then tugged little Peeper's pigtail, and sprung onto the tractor. Milly hurried ahead of the tractor, and pulled open a giant metal gate at the far end of the yard, opening onto the field. As the tractor rumbled through, Burton raised his fingers to his lips, and erupted with an ear splitting whistle. I could not believe what happened then. At least thirty horses appeared on a distant hillside, and in mass, began cantering towards us. I had never seen anything so spectacular in my life. As we drove across the field to a circular wire enclosure, the horses converged upon us. Burton maneuvered the flatbed alongside the metal bin, which I figured out was a feed bin. Mick was already ripping the twine from the bales and tossing the hay into the bin. I followed suit. Hay was flying everywhere, its sweet scent mingled with the smell of horses and fresh air. The horses were frenzied, some kicking others as they jockeyed for position around the feed bin. I was laughing out loud with sheer joy, which I didn't realize until I noticed Mick looking at me incredulously, hands on his hips.

"Are you mental or something?" he asked.

The roar of the tractor drowned any chance of Burton overhearing. He slowly pulled the flatbed around the bin so we could fill it from all sides with the pungent hay. I can still smell that sweet hay wafting across the years, now long gone. Almost nothing on earth smells as wonderful as a bale of fresh hay when you first pull off the twine and it splits open into its succulent neat green sections. Soon the hay was gone and as Burton turned the tractor back to the barn, Mick sat down on the end of the flatbed, legs dangling over the edge, looking back at the horses. I sat down near him, but not *too* near; pretty sure he would have tossed me off the trailer if I were closer. I dangled my legs too, watching the horses. The frenzy had subsided and they circled the bin like spokes of a living wheel, contentedly munching in unison as the autumn sun dipped lower and lower in the sky.

I could not believe so much time had passed already as the tractor pulled back into the yard. It was nearly dinner time. I would need to skedaddle. As I climbed off the flatbed, I noticed that my coat was covered in hay. It stuck everywhere. Tiny red pricks were all over my arms. Great. Allergic to hay. I itched like crazy with the little red welts, but I never gave them more than a moment's thought. It was a small price to pay for such indescribable ecstasy.

Chapter Three

"Today, I will teach you to milk a goat," Milly said.

Stall cleaning and hay unbaling/feeding had been my work for the past two weeks. I had become very proficient at both, though still wobbled like a drunkard when pushing the wheelbarrow. Slowly adding to the load I could successfully manage, my skinny arms were getting stronger.

I had hoped that with my growing competence, Mick might like me a little more, or at least, hate me a little less. That was not to be. If anything, his scorn seemed to accelerate with each passing day. To add to my despair, the buck-toothed girl I had passed on my way to the farm that first day started coming to the farm to volunteer regularly. I don't know if she decided to volunteer after noticing I was obviously working there. She lived in a home just across from the pasture, and perhaps noticed me. She was a little older than me, even skinnier, and in my opinion, ugly. She had stringy mousy brown hair and those enormous teeth. At some point, she got braces. I don't remember if she had them when I first met her or not, but I found I could not look away from her teeth. She reminded me of a horse. Long skinny nose, and huge teeth.

Here is what *really* killed me. Mick loved her. Can you believe it? From the moment Debby showed up, Mick fawned over her. She had no more skill than me and was not as hard a worker. Not even close. I had perfect teeth, by the way. This isn't bragging because I had nothing to do with it. I was just lucky genetically. How could Mick love skinny, buck-toothed, scrawny, limp-haired Debby? I totally didn't get it.

Was it their mutual hatred of me? Debby was as sassy and mean to me as Mick was. They often huddled together, looking my way and laughing.

Anyway, Mick was teaching Debby to ride when Milly pulled me from my stall cleaning duties to teach me to milk the goats. Milly, despite her tough exterior, was never anything but kind to me. She never protected me from her idolized son's taunts, but she herself was always gentle with me.

As we slid into the goat's enclosure, the little kids began butting against me. Some of the older goats had big horns, and as they butted up to me, I backed up to the fence for a getaway. Milly just shoved them away, with a loud noise between clenched teeth.

She grabbed a tricolored goat and looped a rope over her neck. Then she tied the end of the rope to the fence.

"Ok, now this is Cindy. She has taught many kids how to milk, and will be a good one for you to learn on."

Cindy had enormous, full udders. She was the Mae West of goats. I couldn't figure out how the poor thing could walk with those things almost scraping the ground.

Milly grabbed a dirty pail, and put it under the teats. I wondered who planned to drink that goat milk from the dirty pail. Not me, that's for sure. Milly showed me how her thumb and first finger clenched a little higher on the teat to keep the milk from squishing back inside Cindy, and the other fingers moved to push the milk out the spigot. (It isn't really called a spigot, but when you are an effective milker like Milly, it may as well be.)

Cindy stood contentedly, her jaws moving in a circular motion as she chewed her cud. I had never been in close proximity to goats. Just for the record, they stank. At least, these goats did. I had a sensitive nose, and it took some getting used to, sucking in the goat scent.

Anyway, Milly had a waterfall of milk spurting out in no time. As soon as the stream of milk hit the bottom of the pail, it hissed with what was clearly the dinner bell for the farm cats. Cats came streaming out of every tattered building and gathered around Milly. Every so often, she would point the goat's teat at one of the cats, and spew a line of milk right into the cat's open mouth. Her aim was incredible.

"Now you try," she said.

It sure *looked* easy. I positioned my hands just like Milly's had been and squeezed. Placid Cindy kicked me as hard as she could, dumping the pail, and narrowly missing my eye. Ouch. That didn't feel as pleasant as the bucolic scene deserved.

"Not like that," Milly said.

She helped me reposition my hands and put her own rough hands over mine. Cindy was eyeing me with some concern, but she kept her pointy little hooves on the ground. With Milly's help, I began to get the feel of it, and she removed her hands. I could have cheered when the milk hissed into the pail, and the hungry cats moved closer.

Milly stood up and backed away.

"You got it now! Keep milking her until no more comes out. Then we dump the milk in that tin pan over there for the cats."

I smiled, concentrating on my work. Once I had gotten the hang of it, it felt like I had always known how to milk a goat. I was a much better milker than I was a wheel-barrow pusher. In no time, the bucket sloshed half-full of creamy white milk, and Cindy was empty. After pouring the milk in the tin pan for the cats, I stepped back, watching them lap their dinner. Several rumbled like trucks, their purrs were so loud.

Mick rode by on a small horse. Trailing him on a little pony, was Debby. *What!?* I had been working longer than Debby and no one had offered to let *me* on a horse yet! Fuming, I watched them head off on a dusty trail that circled the outer perimeter of the pasture. Debby glanced back at me and smirked. Her giant teeth with their Golden Gate bridge of steel trusses sparkled in the sun. I could not figure it out. What did Mick see in her?

I watched them till they were out of sight, the pit of my stomach dropping even lower than Cindy's enormous kazonkas. Something bubbled inside my head, like vinegar and baking soda had just collided. Capillaries were probably bursting in my eyes. This was so totally unfair. But then, a baby goat suddenly head banged into my thighs. He was so adorable, and as soon as I pushed at him, he pushed back, playing with me. I forgot about Debby and her gleaming horse-teeth. I untied Cindy, and pet her soft muzzle. She closed her eyes dreamily, and nibbled softly at my palm. What a sweet goat. I forgave her the bruise on my cheek.

Milly suddenly appeared, leaning on the fence. Her face had a tender look, with perhaps some pity mingled in.

"Would you like to learn to ride?" she asked.

Had she seem me looking so longingly after Horse-face?? I was embarrassed, but too overjoyed to remember to blush.

"Yes!" I stammered.

"Come with me," she said smiling, "First I'll show you how to put a bridle on Skippy."

Skippy was the tiniest pony ever made. Even pint-sized little Peeper looked average when she was riding Skippy. I was much bigger than Peeper. I figured my legs would nearly be touching the ground on that tiny pony.

"I'm not too big for Skippy?" I asked, "I don't want to hurt him."

"Oh no," laughed Milly, "He's small but he's strong."

While we walked out to the pasture to find Skippy, other workers were gathering the 'trail horses.' They were assorted teens, all volunteers. None were important. I didn't love any of them the way I loved Mick, or hated them more than the manure I shoveled like I hated Debby.

The farm's major income besides boarding the horses was to offer trail rides to the public. Those trail rides were exorbitantly expensive. ('Exorbitant' was a word Mr. Webster and I had a recent meeting over.) I could never understand how anyone would be willing to pay all that money for a slow plodding horse like the sloggers at Burton's Farm. The horses were certainly no beauties, all were old nags, well past their prime. For 47 minutes of the 50 minute trail ride, the horses only walked. There was one three-minute stretch when the horses trotted briefly, not long after starting out. If they trotted on the route *back* to the barn, they might start to canter and no one would be able to stop them. They were *that* anxious to get home and back to their muddy fields and dilapidated stalls.

I could see that section of the trail, across several pastures, where the horses would briefly trot. The riders bobbed about like apples in a bucket of water when the horses trotted. Most were novice riders. Many fell off in that section. It is a wonder that was allowed. Surely some of those people got hurt, but no one ever complained.

The teen workers were the lucky ones that got to lead the trails. Mick was also quite frequently a trail leader. For all his meanness, he was an incredible rider. He never used a saddle. In fact, none of the trail leaders did. The saddles were needed for the paying customers. There was always one worker leading and then one following the trail. If someone fell off and his horse ran away, which happened way more often than it probably should have, the follower would first make sure the person was still alive and unharmed.

If so, the follower would next attempt to snag the horse as it tried to dash back to the barn. When that attempt failed, as it often did, the follower would sometimes walk the fallen rider back to the barn. Sometimes the follower would just point the disgraced rider in the right direction and then trot off to join the others. I don't know if they refunded the fallen rider's money or not. I'm guessing…not. I saw that happen dozens of times, while milking the goats or tossing hay to the horses.

As Milly led me off to catch Skippy, the teens haltered the trail horses and lined them up along the fence. Then they busily saddled and bridled them. Mick and Debby had returned, and out of the corner of my eye, I saw Mick kiss Debby briefly.

Oh, ick. On so many levels that repulsed me. First, how could he kiss that ugly face? Secondly, how could he kiss her and not be lacerated by all that hardware? And ooh-ick, much as I loved Mick, at age nine the idea of kissing *anyone* on the mouth was disgusting to me. My romantic inclinations only involved having him be *nice* to me, and maybe let me toss hay alongside him without him making fun of my frizzy hair or muteness in his presence.

Milly nickered like a horse. As if by magic, little Skippy trotted toward us. Milly slipped the halter over his tiny head and showed me how to snap on the lead line, and then lead Skippy to the barn. The last twenty feet or so of the field up to the barn door was a particular challenge. Because the horses milled about in that area, waiting to come into the barn, it was heavily trampled mud. The water trough was near there, and it was always leaking. So the mud was at least a foot deep, and like quicksand. I sank up to my knees. Little horses like Skippy had a lot of trouble wading through that morass. Each step they took required enormous effort, as with a great sucking noise, they wrenched their foot out of the mud to move forward. Some horses injured their hocks trying to pull their heavy hooves out of that muck. In autumn, as it was when I started at the farm, it was not too bad. Spring with the winter melt was the worst time of the year for this. Somehow, Skippy and I plunged through the terrible mud and made it safely into the barn.

Milly showed me where the bucket of brushes and curry combs were. She tied Skippy's lead rope to a metal ring riveted to the wall and began brushing his back. In the same way I had learned to brush a dog in the direction the hair lay, Milly brushed from withers toward rump. Unlike the goat smells which were not as nasty as manure, but not by any stretch *pleasant*, horses had an earthy smell of wind and fields. It evoked ancient memories of open plains and endless skies with enormous herds of buffalo. Not that *I* had those memories. Maybe they were coded into the human DNA. In short, I liked the way horses smelled.

"That's all there is to brushing," said Milly, snapping me from my musings of the wild, wild West.

She handed me the brush. I finished Skippy's back and was working on his neck when Milly returned with the bridle.

"Oh you just need to do his back," she said, "Just where you sit so you don't rub a burr or anything into him."

No wonder poor Skippy looked so bedraggled. I suspected no one ever bothered to brush him, or *any* of the horses, except where the saddle perched.

Speaking of the saddle, Milly didn't remember it, at least none were in sight. She showed me how to bridle. That was interesting. She stuck her thumb and first finger on either side of Skippy's mouth, and squeezed. Skippy's mouth popped open and Milly snuck the bit in before

Skippy knew what was happening. Then she pulled the leather straps up and secured the top behind his ears. She handed me the reins and unhooked the lead rope.

"Let's go," she said.

"What about the saddle?" I asked.

"Oh, you learn to ride without a saddle. Then you develop the balance you need to ride anything."

I was dubious, but I was not going to argue, or blow this opportunity. As I was leading Skippy out of the barn, Mick walked by, leading a dark brown horse. The horse had wild eyes, ringed in white. Mick had a firm grip on the halter lead, and was roughly jerking the horse's head so he would stop his prancing and side-stepping. The horse looked terrified. He was a small horse, several hands shorter than the trail horses. He had a mix of brown and black in his coat, with a mottled effect. His tail and mane were thick, and like all the horses there, tangled and covered with burrs.

Trail riders were starting to arrive now and workers were finishing preparing the trail horses for the riders. Girths were being tightened, bridles latched, stirrups lowered.

Milly put her hand on my shoulder as we reached the center of the yard. She cupped her hands and said, "Put your left knee in my hands and I'll help you up."

I did. It was the wrong knee.

Mick glanced over and guffawed, "Your *other* left knee, doofus."

I have always struggled with knowing my right and left. I used to suck my thumb, way past the time I should have. (My mom finally had to paint it with nasty stuff called Bitter Apple to get me to stop.) Anyway, I knew I sucked my right thumb, and so when someone asked me to do something involving right or left choices, I held up my thumbs to see which one I wanted to suck. In this case, I didn't have time, and so made a wild guess. I was wrong.

Milly tapped my other knee, the real left knee. I bent my leg and stuck my knee in her hand. She hoisted me up and I swung my right leg across Skippy's back. I was on a horse! Heaven! My bottom settled into the gentle curve of Skippy's back, just behind the withers. I could feel the heat of him through my thighs, and felt the rhythmic expansion of his sides as he breathed. While he was a tiny pony, I felt like I had scaled a mountain. What a view from atop a horse!

Mick was struggling with the dark little horse who was snorting and side-stepping as he bridled him. Still, he was glancing at me and shaking his head in disdain.

"Loser," he muttered.

Milly put the reins over Skippy's head and into my hand.

"Now you hold them in one hand, like this. If you want to go left, you bring both reins to the right over his neck. To stop, you pull back and say, "Ho." To go, you kick him with your heels. That's all there is to it."

I nodded. She looked at me, her blue-grey eyes expectant. A moment passed.

"Well...go. Kick him."

I did, very gently. The idea of kicking any living creature seemed cruel.

Skippy didn't budge.

"Harder," said Milly.

I did. A little harder.

Mick was still watching and shaking his head. He had bridled the horse, and now catapulted into the air and onto the horse's back. I couldn't believe how graceful that incredible feat was. The horse seemed less impressed. He gave a wild snort and began bucking. Mick had spurs on, and he began digging his spurs in the poor horse's sides. The horse bucked and twisted two more times and then bolted forward. He raced onto the dusty trail and galloped the full length of the fence. Then Mick reined him around, kicked his heaving sides savagely, and galloped him back. He pulled the horse to a screaming stop at the yard edge. The horse was dripping sweat, and a white lather foamed from his mouth, and flew through the air as he tossed his head.

"Ho, Joe!" Mick barked, pulling back with all his strength on the poor horse's reins. Joe, the horse, backed up ten feet, shaking his head, foam spewing all over his dark chest.

By now, the trail riders were all lined up, and mounted on their ragged steeds. Milly explained to them that Mick would be the leader, and I would be the follower.

What??

I, who had never, not once, been on a horse, was to be the one to catch runaway horses, and help any dumped riders back up. Perhaps the trail riders were not incredulous, but I sure was. My mouth dropped open, and my eyes became more wild than the bucking black horse Mick rode. That was nothing compared to the expression on Mick's face.

Chapter Four

I think Mick was about to erupt in a string of invectives, but for once, Milly stifled him. She held up a warning hand, and nodded to him to move out.

He swirled the dark, sweating Joe around, and started off down the trail. Joe pranced, eyes still ringed in white. I didn't know much about horses, but I knew that Mick was cruel, and that poor Joe was scared. The teens led the other riders in tandem to the trail head, and then slapped the horse's rump. With a groan, each tired, old horse plodded behind the one in front of it.

As the last horse rounded the corner onto the trail, Milly led me forward on Skippy.

"If you feel like you are losing your balance, just grab a hold of Skippy's mane," she advised. *If?* I grabbed Skippy's mane.

Gulping, I nodded. She smacked Skippy's rump. A cloud of dust rose up, from its long established lair in the rarely brushed nether regions. It clogged my nostrils temporarily, drifting like a swarm of gnats around me, and adding a gritty flavor to my fears. With that, we were off. Fortunately, Skippy was disinclined to put forth much effort, and plodded at a peaceful walk, well behind the last horse. It was a bit terrifying at first, I'll admit. I had never been on a horse, and had never been known as physically proficient in...well...anything. Gripping the mane with white knuckles, I tried to remember what Milly had told me about how to steer.

The first mile of the trail ride was not bad at all. I gripped Skippy's mane like it was the last piece of candy at Halloween (which being one of four greedy children was not an easy feat in my family, and one learned to develop a strong grip.) His hooves sang a comforting clip-clop song that had a higher timbre than the clip-clop of the larger horses in front of us. The horses in front of me raised a thick fog of swirling dirt that settled like a fine coat of powder all over me. I sneezed, and Skippy snapped his ears back. Even at a walk, my weight was shifted dramatically back and forth, my pelvis pivoting in cadence to Skippy's stride. The smell of dried fallen leaves along the trail, mingled with horse sweat. Occasionally, a horse in front of me raised his tail, and dropped huge balls of poop with resounding plops. I couldn't get over how they would just keep walking while pooping. That seemed uncomfortable at best...not that I'd ever tried it myself. The inside of my thighs ached within minutes. It was clear I had never used those muscles for much of anything before, and they were not entirely happy about it.

The horses plodded along, nose to tail of the horse before them. Joe, at the lead, was still prancing and side-stepping, and even occasionally bucking. Mick clung to him like a leech. I hated that Mick was so rough on poor Joe, but had to admire his ability to stay on. Some of the horses stopped and munched on some grass along the way. Mick occasionally turned around and screamed at me to tell the riders to pull the horses' heads up. I largely ignored him because frankly, it took all my concentration to remain on Skippy's back.

We rounded the corner where the horses all got to do their three-minute trot. The riders in front of me grabbed hold of their saddle horns, and as each horse sputtered into a slow trot, the riders bobbled about with heads snapping like popcorn on their necks. Finally, the wave of trotters trickled back to Skippy. With a grunt, he started trotting.

Some horses have smooth trots. I have heard them described as "rocking horses." This is not even close to how I would describe Skippy's trot. Skippy's trot was more like riding a series of firecrackers, all being fired at different times. I clutched his mane and felt my teeth all crunching so forcefully against each other that I feared for my perfect bite. As if in slow motion, I felt myself losing my balance. Now that is not quite accurate, since in reality, I had never had any balance to lose.

I started to slip sideways. I gripped my legs as tightly as I could around Skippy's slippery hair, and slowly, I began to tilt. I gripped harder. This is hard to believe, but I actually flipped upside down, and was hanging under Skippy's belly, with my legs still clenched around his midsection. My head was between his front legs, and I was holding on for dear life.

NO one can keep that position for long. Trust me on this. After a few seconds in this compromising position, I let go. I had to. Unable to cling any longer to the underbelly of a pony, I crashed to the ground. Miraculously, not a single one of his hooves crushed my skull.

I ate a few mouthfuls of dirt as the cavalcade disappeared in the distance. When Skippy realized he was 'sans rider', he stopped. He turned and looked at me, lying in the dust, then cantered home.

I sat up. Mick never looked back, as far as I knew. If he did, he probably figured *good riddance.* Any way about it, he didn't stop to try to help me. I stood up, and checked to see if all my parts worked. A little bruised, but nothing seemed broken. With a sigh, I headed back to the barn, following the dust of the carefree Skippy.

Milly was standing at the trail head, holding Skippy's reins, when I finally trudged to the farm yard. She looked relieved when she saw me.

"Skippy came home without you," she said.

I nodded. I refrained from saying, *Thank you, Captain Obvious.*

"Are you hurt?"

"No."

"Would you like to try again? This time in the riding ring?"

I nodded again, and followed her to the ring.

She held out her cupped hands, and this time, I put the correct left knee in her hands. She hoisted me onto Skippy's back and handed me the reins.

"Just walk for a few laps," she suggested.

She opened the metal gate to the riding ring, and led Skippy in.

"I have some work I need to do," she said, letting go of the reins, "but I'll shut the gate so you just practice as long as you like. Call me if you need help. I think you will do just fine."

You do? I was not so sure, but I smiled weakly, and nodded. Skippy slowly walked forward, along the ring perimeter. I began to grow accustomed to his cadence, the roll of his shoulders and back with each step. After one lap, he stopped at the gate. I gently kicked him. Nothing. No acknowledgement of my polite request for him to keep moving at all.

So I kicked him harder. Still nothing, except an irritated flick of his ear. Now I was getting mad. I was doing everything in my power to be nice to the pony, and he was definitely abusing my kindness.

So I kicked him with my heels as hard as I could. Both his ears snapped back, and he lurched forward. I slid back towards his rump as he broke into the teeth splitting trot that had knocked me off of him the first time. Fortunately, I was still gripping his mane, and managed to pull myself back onto the dip in his back where I belonged. My arms were flapping, legs flailing with each jarring step, and my bottom flying four inches up and then smacking down. It was not exactly fun, but I hung on. There were some close calls, but I made it all the way around the ring without falling off.

Skippy stopped at the gate, though I had not strictly asked him to. Nonetheless, I was relieved. I petted his neck, and said, "Good boy, Skippy."

He turned to look at me. He nibbled at my knee and then turned his head forward again. I think he was letting me know that there were no hard feelings. I held my heels against his side, and nudged. Not a kick, just a nudge.

Surprisingly, he stepped forward.

"Thank you," I whispered, petting his neck, which took a lot of courage, because I had to let go of his mane to do so. We circled the ring several times, at the peaceful walk. I noticed Mick and the trail riders returning, and saw Mick glance over at me. He rolled his eyes, then spurred Joe and cantered into the yard, out of sight. The teen helpers assisted the riders off their horses, and led the tired nags to the water trough.

I knew it was time for me to be heading home, but I had a problem. The only way I knew to get off a horse was to fall off. Skippy pulled up to the gate and waited. I sat on his back considering this new dilemma. It's not that I was super high off the ground. It's just that I had never done a dismount. How does one get off a horse?

I noticed Mick peeking around the corner. When he saw me look up, he darted away. Fortunately, Big-Tooth Debby wasn't around. I suspected she had already gone home.

With a sigh, I leaned forward onto Skippy's neck, and after several tries, managed to pull my right leg up and onto his rump. I would've been fine, but he started to fidget and I tumbled off onto my side with a thud. Skippy looked down and nuzzled my hair. He blew a stream of warm air onto my aching head.

I reached up and pet his muzzle.

"Wow, I think you should enter our next horse show," Mick said.

How long had he been watching? I heaved to my feet, and smacked the dust off my pants.

"Maybe you could be the clown," he said.

I didn't look at him, but gathered Skippy's reins, and pulled open the gate. Mick stepped aside as I silently led the pony past him. He was still laughing softly. I looked straight ahead, and batted my eyes. I would not cry. A tiny tear may have trickled out of my eye, but Mick had disappeared around the back corner of the barn and didn't see it.

I walked into the yard, leading Skippy behind me. Joe, the horse Mick had been riding, stood tied to the fence. His head hung low, and he looked depressed.

I found Milly and asked what I should do with Skippy. She helped me unbridle him and lead him back to the mud booby trap just out the back door. She smacked his rump, and he trotted off into the field.

"How did it go?" she asked.

"I stayed on," I said. No need to mention the dismount.

"Good for you!"

"I have to go now," I said, "I'm sorry I didn't help with the feeding today."

Milly paused, pushing a stray flop of hair out of her eyes. She always had her long hair in a single braid that streamed halfway down her back.

"You did a good day's work already, and for two weeks have been the hardest worker we have. You deserved some fun."

I smiled back at her.

"Milly," I said, summoning my courage, "That horse, Joe. The one Mick was on. Why does he buck like that?"

Milly sighed.

"No one can ride Joe at all except Mick. And that's just because Mick is hard to buck off. We got Joe from an owner that was cruel to him. His mouth was torn to pieces from rough handling with the bit. Now, he refuses to take a bit at all. We use a hackamore on him – that's a bridle without the bit. He nearly killed us when we tried to get a saddle on him. If we even walk near with a saddle, he starts kicking and biting. He's a mean horse, but I don't think he started off that way in life. We had thought we could use him for a trail horse, but, well, that didn't work out."

I looked out the front of the barn to the fence where Joe was tied. His head still hung close to the ground, and his ears were back.

"See his ears," she said.

I nodded.

"When a horse has his ears back like that, it means he's not happy. Always be careful to watch a horse's ears."

"Why isn't he happy now?" I asked.

"He's ornery. Joe is never happy. I don't like what Mick does to him when he rides, but the only way Joe is of use to us here at all is if he can be a lead horse for the trails."

I gazed again at Joe, his despondency breaking my heart.

"Would it be ok if I brushed him?" I asked.

Milly looked steadily at me, as though she could see inside my skull. I suspect in a way she could.

"He's mean, Vicky. It would not be a good idea for you to go near him."

"Can I try? If he puts his ears back or looks like he's going to kick me, I won't go near."

Milly stood quietly, and I was afraid she hadn't heard me. Then she reached in her pocket and pulled out a horse treat.

"Here. Offer him this. You hold your hand flat like this. Keep your fingers straight and out of your palm so he doesn't bite them."

I grabbed a soft brush from the brush bin, and took the horse treat. Then slowly, and silently, I walked toward the dark horse. Approaching him, I spoke very quietly.

"Hi Joe. I'm Vicky. You're a good boy, Joe. Good horse, Joe." I didn't have much experience with horses, but had always loved animals, and they seemed to like me. Joe glanced at me, and one of his ears flicked forward as I held out my hand with the treat in my palm. I moved forward step by step, my hand stretched out before me, watching his ears.

I paused just a few steps from him, so that if he stretched out his neck he could reach me. My arm was still outstretched, palm open, fingers flat just like Milly had told me. He lifted his head. I watched his ears. Both ears now flicked forward. I didn't speak, in fact, I don't think I breathed for fear of spooking him.

He stretched his muzzle towards me and very gently nibbled the treat from my hand. His muzzle was so soft. Nothing is as soft as a horse's muzzle.

I stood there watching him as he munched the treat. He watched me, too, and not unkindly. We had made a connection. So I stepped forward one step, watching his ears. They remained forward. I took another step, and was now close enough to touch his neck. Slowly, slowly, I raised my hand and stroked his neck. He didn't move at all. His ears flicked but they didn't snap backwards like they'd been before.

I don't know how long I stood there petting his neck, but knew I would be late for dinner. It didn't matter. Nothing mattered but the communion with this horse. Finally, I remembered the brush, and began brushing his neck. There were huge clumps of mud and dirt all over him. His mane was a tangled mess. As I brushed his neck, he closed his eyes.

For the next twenty minutes or so, I worked my way from his neck, to his withers, to his rump. He stood stock still, occasionally opening his eyes, but mostly standing quietly as I brushed him. I didn't want to leave, but as though emerging from a dream, realized the sun was dipping very low in the sky. It was time to go.

I moved to his face and stroked his cheek. He looked at me, and I knew we had an understanding.

"Goodbye, Joe," I whispered, "Tomorrow maybe we can untangle your mane."

He nuzzled my arm. As I turned back to the barn to return the brush, I noticed Mick across the yard, a bucket of grain for the goats dangling from his hand. He was watching me, and for once, hatred was not etched in his face. As soon as I glanced at him, he turned away, and I wasn't sure if I had imagined the softness I thought I'd seen in his expression for a flicker of a second.

Chapter Five

I had been working at the farm for a month. The days grew shorter and colder. The times I cherished the most were the brief moments I could steal with Joe. Every day that I had a spare minute, I would try to spend it with him. I was determined that the sour, lonely horse would have at least one friend on Burton's Farm.

When I trudged through the mud and out to the field, he ignored me. I crept closer and closer holding out my hand with whatever enticing snack I had brought from home for him. Usually it was apple slices or carrots. He was always alone in the same section of the field. He didn't like the other horses, and they were wary of him. If they came near, he bared his teeth and lunged at them. Equines and humans alike shunned Joe. So, I never had to fight off other horses to get near him. He liked to stand near a crabapple tree alongside a small pond in a field to the right and just behind the barn. A sagging lean-to was near the spot, and that's where the outdoor horses hid from the hot sun or rain. The field horses were never brought in the barn. Even in the worst storms, their only protection was the lean-to.

Despite initially pretending I wasn't there, he never seemed aggressive or mean. Mostly, at first, he just seemed indifferent. For the first couple of days, I stood at a distance, talking to him in a soft voice. He perked his ears forward listening. I told him about my day at school, and about the pictures I was drawing or the stories I was writing. I don't think I had anything very interesting to say, particularly if judged by Mick's reaction.

"Marshmallow brain," he shouted, surprising me one day from behind, "Are you out here talking to yourself? Not surprised since no one wants to talk to you."

I swung around. I didn't want to tell him I was talking to Joe. That might incur double derision. Besides, I didn't want him to notice Joe. I hated it when he would catch Joe in the field and lead him so roughly, and then ride him so cruelly. By parking myself between him and Joe, there was a chance he wouldn't see Joe and choose a different horse to lead the trail.

As usual, I couldn't come up with a single retort, so just blinked at him mutely. Mick then brought a cigarette to his mouth, and puffed. Ah, he was here to sneak a smoke. I didn't want him to die of lung cancer, but it was a far better fate than that which awaited poor Joe when he rode him.

"Want a drag?" he asked.

I shook my head. Frankly, I was surprised he'd asked. That may be the nicest thing he'd ever said to me. I almost wished I partook of that deadly, nasty habit.

"Figures." He turned and headed away, downfield from the barn and Milly's prying eyes. I turned back to Joe. He had moved to the far side of the pond, obviously to get as far away as possible from Mick. His ears were back, and the skin along his shoulders trembled.

Over the next few days, I was able to move closer and closer. Then one day, I stood still, holding out a carrot, and a miracle occurred. Joe walked up to me! He came over, sniffing loudly through flared nostrils, a friendly look on his face, and took the carrot right off my palm. While he crunched the carrot, I petted his neck.

"Hey Joe, so much happened today. When the teacher called on me, I thought my heart would pop right out of my chest, but I answered the question right. She even told me I was 'very perceptive.' I wasn't sure what that meant at first, but I looked it up. I had a feeling it was good from the way she smiled at me. I was right. It means I have insights."

Joe chewed the carrot, listening.

"And then, when I was standing in line for lunch, Robert told me my slip was showing."

I paused, remembering my humiliation.

"I told him that was not my slip, but just the way my dress was made. I don't think he believed me. I wanted to die, Joe, but then I remembered you would be here waiting for me. And who would feed you a carrot if I died? No one, that's who."

Joe gazed at me, with a 'perceptive' look on his face. Now that I knew what that word meant, it applied perfectly to Joe.

From that day forward, when I walked into the field, Joe came to meet me. I started bringing a brush, and a curry comb so I could spend a few minutes working on the impossible tangles. Slowly, I was unsnarling the mess of tangles in his tail. It would take months before both his mane and tail were clear of knots.

I'd become a valuable worker by now. My jobs included: prepping the trail horses by brushing them, finding their bridles and saddles, carrying the tack and placing it near the correct horse, and taking the riders' checks to Milly. When the trail riders moved off for their ride, I milked the goats, fed the cats, mucked the stalls, and unbaled and tossed the hay.

"I think you are ready to move on from milking the goats to milking Matilda now," Milly said. Now, my skill set would advance further! I'd learn to milk the cow!

Matilda was an enormous cow, and a mixed up one at that. She had an unnerving habit of mounting unsuspecting people. Milly explained that in the absence of other cows or bulls, Matilda seemed to think she was a bull. I don't know if Matilda's behavior was normal, but it was certainly frightening. I'd seen her try to mount Mick, and even the fearless tyrant Mick was scared of her.

So I am sure my eyes registered terror, even to someone not as perceptive as Milly.

"Don't worry," she said, "We will be sure you never approach Matilda unless she is tied. I'll stay with you till you feel confident. But I have an even bigger surprise."

Bigger than Matilda, the biggest cow I'd ever seen? I waited, hoping it was a more pleasant surprise than milking a sexually confused, over-sized cow.

"You have been with us a month now. That means, you have earned the right to your own horse. As long as you work here, you can choose a horse that is yours alone to ride and take care of. Except of course, when we need him for trails. As long as none of the other workers have claimed him, you may choose any horse. One of the older, gentler ones would be a good horse to start with."

I was speechless, which was actually not that unusual. Even my thoughts slammed to a stop for a moment from the shock. This was a bonus beyond belief. I had still only ridden little Skippy. I was getting better, but I was not slipping into anything approaching competence yet. I'd never been on a horse at this point. When I was astraddle little Skippy, my feet were no more than a foot off the ground.

"Think about which horse you'd like," she said, "and then let me know."

"Joe," I said instantly, regaining use of my vocal cords.

"Joe?"

"Yes, I want Joe."

"Vicky, you don't want Joe. No one can ride Joe, except Mick. Joe is mean. You'll never be able to ride him. How about Beauty? She is a really gentle horse, and a good one to learn on."

Beauty was indeed gentle. She was the horse little Peeper usually rode. Should I be insulted that the horse I was being offered was one the five-year-old could handle?

"No," I said, with a firmness that surprised me at least as much as it did Milly, "I want Joe. I will keep riding Skippy to learn, but I want Joe to be my horse."

Milly laughed and shook her head, "Well then, Joe it is."

"Does that mean Mick won't ride him anymore?" I asked. I knew it was a bit presumptuous of me to ask this, but I wanted more than anything that poor Joe would never be subjected to Mick's cruel spurs again.

Milly sighed. "I can't promise that, Vicky. Sometimes we need Joe for a trail leader."

I looked at her, not turning away. To maintain eye contact with anyone for any length of time was a terrible trial to me, but I kept my eyes steadily on her face, not speaking.

"I'll try," she said finally, "When we don't *have* to use Joe, I'll try to have Mick ride another horse."

I smiled at her.

"Now, are you ready to learn how to milk Matilda?" she asked.

I nodded, but I was not. However, I *was* ready to leap out of my skin. Joe was mine! *My own horse,* at least as long as I worked at Burton's

Farm, which would be *forever*. Milly, completely oblivious to my turmoil, grabbed a pail and handed me a bucket.

"Two buckets?" I questioned.

"One to sit on."

We headed to Matilda's stall. She was quietly chewing hay as we approached.

"As with any animal," Milly advised, "always speak to her as you come from behind so you don't startle her. She will not kick if she knows you are there."

Matilda turned her head, and looked at us with solemn brown eyes, placidly chewing her cud.

Taking my bucket, Milly flopped it upside down and sat down on it, aligned with Matilda's udders. She flipped her long braid over her shoulder so it lay neatly down the center of her back. She positioned her pail under the udders.

"It's pretty much like milking the goats," she said, and proceeded to show me.

Just like the goat milking session, cats began appearing like flies to honey. They came from every corner of the barn. Within nanoseconds, cats materialized whenever milk spurted from a teat.

Milly demonstrated a few brief squirts, then stood up.

"Your turn."

I sat on the overturned bucket and began milking. Milly was correct. It was not much different than milking Cindy. It was actually easier because the teats themselves were longer and easier to get a hold of.

She watched me for a few moments, and then asked, "Do you feel comfortable now?"

"I'm fine," I agreed.

She patted me on the back, and left me alone. The cats remained prowling about me as I milked. It was very peaceful, the only sound the milk hissing as it hit the metal pail bottom. I don't know where the other workers were. Sometimes they would all disappear into the field, and I would be alone. Milly and Burton were usually around, but not always. There were thousands of chores on that little farm, and some took place in the sheds across the yard. I had little to do with the chickens or the pigs, which all lived in that section. I really only ventured over there to milk Cindy. Zeke, the watch dog, was tied near that area, so I didn't explore that half of the yard very much. I assumed the rest of the gang was over there. I suspected some of those teens, including Mick, smoked cigarettes, as I'd seen flashes of them doing so when Burton and Milly drove off on errands. Maybe that's what everyone was busy doing while I milked Matilda.

Speaking of that section of the farm, there was another reason I rarely traipsed over there. I had never yet seen the stallion, who was housed in a shed in that section. He made his presence known often enough, neighing or kicking the walls. The mysterious stallion terrified me almost as much as the dog. There were rumors the stallion had killed a man. The only one that could handle him was Burton, and even Burton would clear the yard when he brought the stallion out. I don't recall the stallion ever being loose in the field, though surely he must have been from time to time. Poor stallion. Living most of one's life in a tiny shed seemed to me a miserable existence. I'd be kicking down the walls too, if I were him.

While enjoying the silence, I finished milking Matilda and poured the milk into a silver pan for the cats. Matilda again looked back at me, her dark eyes gentle with long eyelashes hooding them.

I sidled alongside her, until reaching her head.

"Hello Matilda. Thanks for letting me milk you." I smiled at her sweet face, and ran my knuckles gently down her forehead.

Quicker than a robin yanking a worm, Matilda hopped on me. Her front legs somehow came up around my shoulders, while her head rested on my own. Honestly, I can't imagine how she was able to do that while tethered, but she did. I screamed. What a cruel way to die, crushed by a horny cow.

She must not have put her full weight on me, because I seriously doubt I would have lived. Out of nowhere, I heard a deep growling voice, and saw a figure leap from the aisle by the manger at Matilda's head. Wild waving arms helicoptered across her face and somehow, she was shoved off of me. I scrambled out of the stall, tripping over the pan of cat milk, sprawling to the floor as I clutched my heart.

Flopping onto my bottom in a less than graceful heap, I exhaled as the wind was knocked out of me. I gasped for breath. Mick stood in the aisle by the manger glaring at me. Then he burst into laughter, and disappeared as quickly as he had appeared. I heard him muttering, "Imbecile."

Mick had just saved my life. And then, as usual, mocked me. I sat on the floor, partially covered in sweet, sticky milk. Tears trickled out of the corner of my eyes. Then I felt a rough, raspy tongue licking my milk-spotted arms. The barn cats gathered around me, their ministrations slowly dissolving my humiliation and fear.

Vicky Kaseorg

Chapter Six

Milly's style of working with me was very similar to my mom's. Benign Neglect. I don't recall ever having another lesson in riding after her initial help with Skippy. From that moment forward, anything I learned, I learned by trial and error. It may not surprise anyone to know it was mostly by error. The good news: I was a rich source of entertainment for Mick and Debby. They often meandered by when I led Skippy to the riding ring, and then they sat on the fence to watch me.

Determined not to be cowed by their presence, I worked hard to ignore them. It wasn't easy because they kept up a running commentary on my skill, or lack thereof.

"Notice how she bounces high enough to see the Empire State building between the saddle and her bottom?" Mick said, "Not everyone can keep that much distance between the horse and rider without breaking out of Earth's atmosphere."

Pithy comments like that.

Without Milly to give me a knee up, I first had to learn to get on Skippy all by myself. You would not think this would be hard for me since

I was taller than Skippy. You would be wrong. I leaped and grunted and threw myself as high into the air as I could and then flopped across his back like a beached whale, trying mightily to flip my leg across him. This caused peals of laughter to erupt from Monster Teeth and Mick. My face flamed bright red, but I kept trying. Finally, I had to lead him to the mounting block, which only the little kids used.

"Baby!" Mick mocked, as I clambered up the steps, and crawled onto Skippy's back.

Even Little Peeper could pull herself onto a pony without the mounting block. What was perhaps even more demoralizing was Little Peeper, at age five, often rode one of the biggest horses at the farm. Her legs barely straddled him, he was so wide. She looked like a little ragdoll way up on top of the giant horse. Her legs stuck straight out. Yet somehow, she managed to kick him hard enough that he would go, and had the strength to pull on the reins to make him stop. She utterly amazed me. And humbled me. Bested by a foul-mouthed five-year-old. That did wonders for my confidence.

I practiced trotting without falling off for weeks before I dared canter. The first time I rode Skippy at a canter was by accident. He startled at a passing car back-firing and broke into a canter. After I stuffed my heart back in my chest, I was pleasantly surprised to discover that a canter is a much more comfortable gait to ride than a trot. It really is like a rocking horse. It is fast, and so I almost psyched myself out. When I didn't fall off, I relaxed. Soon, I was eagerly and almost skillfully cantering around the ring. I was actually happy that Mick and the Toothsome One were watching me that day. When it was obvious I was not going to do anything taunt-worthy, Tyrannosaurus Teeth nudged Mick and they left. I almost never fell off, and just as Milly promised, was developing decent balance and a steady seat. Thus, I bored them, and they lost interest.

Even more importantly, having learned of Joe's history and having watched Mick see-sawing with such cruelty on Joe's reins, I was determined to always have "soft hands." I never wanted to be responsible for cutting up or bruising a horse's delicate mouth. So I worked very hard at using the reins gently, to guide as minimally as necessary.

As autumn gave way to winter, many of the farm workers dropped away. Chicago winters were brutal. There were squalls that dumped three feet of snow at a time. Temperatures were often in the single digits. None of that deterred me. I don't ever recall feeling cold. I never missed a day racing to the farm after school, unless I was sick. I cannot remember any time in my life being so utterly consumed with joy. Nothing was more wonderful than Burton's Farm to my shy, introverted, horse-crazy self.

Milly allowed me to bring Joe into the barn on those bitter cold days while I worked. I tied him to the metal rings in the main barn, and brushed him till his coat shone. Well, okay, that's not true. His shaggy winter coat never exactly *shone*, but it was mud free, and that was no small accomplishment. I went about my work, but every few minutes stopped to chat with Joe, feed him a treat from my pocket, and spend some time nuzzling against his warm neck. There were no trail rides over the winter months, so the workers had more spare time than in the warmer weather.

It was that first winter that Milly told me more about Joe's history. He was a hackney pony, which is defined as under 58-inches at the withers. Hackneys were specifically bred to be cart horses. Milly told me that Joe used to win prizes as a cart horse. She must have noticed the gleam in my eye, because she asked me if I would like to learn how to "drive" Joe in a cart.

Would I ever!!

"Do you have a cart?" I asked.

She smiled at me, and nodded, a faraway look in her eye. The cart had not been used in many years.

"Come with me," she said.

She led me to a shed, filled with old tools, and rusted machinery. Along one wall was a cart. It was covered in cobwebs and dust. Hanging on a nail on the wall above the cart was the harness. The leather was worn and weathered, even cracked in places with some of the stitching pulling apart. Milly yanked the harness down from the wall and handed it to me. I sneezed, and dust motes sparkled in the air. There was a bridle with long reins, which she also piled into my arms. Then she grabbed the long shafts of the cart, and wheeled it out of the shed. Together we proceeded to the barn.

Joe was, as usual, tied to the barn wall. He had been munching hay, but glanced up with interest as the cart was wheeled in. Milly stopped beside him and lowered the arms of the cart to the floor. Joe sniffed it, ears perked forward.

"He looks interested," I said.

Milly took the harness from my hands and approached Joe. He backed away and snorted. She glanced at me.

"May I try?" I asked.

She showed me how the straps should lie across Joe's back, and handed me the heavy, complicated load. Harnessing is a little difficult, but with Milly talking me through it, I managed. To Milly's amazement, Joe stood stock still. He let me strap everything in place.

"That horse trusts you," she said.

And I trusted him. Joe and I were best friends. He knew everything about me by now…everything that mattered.

With the harness in place, Milly now maneuvered the cart behind Joe, and showed me how to attach it to the harness. Joe stood quietly, like he did this every day. Milly helped me put the bridle on Joe's head. It was not really a bridle, but a hackamore, without a bit. She wove the long reins through the traces and brought them over his back, and laid them on the seat of the cart.

"Ready?"

I gaped at her.

"It's easy to drive a cart," she said, "You direct the horse by pulling on the reins on the side you want him to turn to. Pull back on both reins to stop him. To make him go, you slap the reins down on his rump."

There was a long whip in the cart.

"If you want him to trot, you flick the end of this whip on his rump. It's easy, and Joe used to be a champion cart horse. I bet you anything, he will remember."

I untied Joe, and led him into the yard. He lifted his head high, arcing his neck as though he were a prize horse, and not an old shaggy nag. He almost pranced, as the cart rolled behind him. Milly held him still as I climbed into the cart.

"Good luck," she said, letting go of the reins.

I flicked the reins down gently on Joe's rump.

"Get up," I said.

Joe stepped forward, tossing his head, his newly combed mane flowing.

"Just follow the trail," Milly called.

I pulled on the left reins, and Joe turned onto the trail.

"Have him trot!" Milly yelled.

I slapped the reins on his rump. "Trot, Joe."

Without hesitation, Joe sprang forward in a trot. His head lifted in the frosty air, his nostrils blowing a stream of wispy fog behind him. His beautiful tail arched and streamed like a banner in his wake. I laughed with delight as the little cart bounced over the frozen dirt. The beautiful pony stretched his old legs, and perhaps remembered his youth for a moment.

Chapter Seven

"You are a natural cart driver," Milly said.

I blushed.

"You know, every few months, we sponsor a horse show. Cart driving is one of the classes. I think you would do well in that class."

"But I just learned."

"You have several months to practice. Besides that, there are usually very few entrants. Sometimes only one horse enters the cart class."

Now that was intriguing. I had an excellent chance at a ribbon.

I could not practice driving the cart too much, since it took so much time to get Joe ready and harnessed. When I did have time, usually on a Saturday, I discovered that Joe was an excellent cart horse. He enjoyed it as much as I did. He always seemed to lift his head a little higher and arch his neck and his tail a little more proudly. Despite my complete lack of experience as a driver, Joe never was anything but perfect in the traces.

One day, as usual after our cart session, I polished him with special brushing. His winter coat was very shaggy and thick, but soon, he was clean of mud and dirt. I wanted to clean his ankles, but as yet, had never brushed his lower legs. Mick was grumpily cleaning a stall nearby. Mick never smiled during barn work.

"Can I brush his ankles?" I asked Milly.

"Ankles!" Mick shouted, "Did you call his fetlocks *ankles*? Are you from Mars?"

I am not sure if he expected an answer. Personally, I don't think Martians are the only ones that don't know they are not called ankles, but that insight didn't keep the shame from creeping over me like a tsunami.

Anyway, Milly was a little concerned because Joe was so crotchety. She thought if I fiddled with his legs, he might put a hoof through my skull. I knew he wouldn't, and told her so.

Milly again gazed at me, as though my head was transparent and there was something inside she needed to have a closer look at. Then she nodded, but told me to watch his ears. She also warned that if he started stomping his feet, I should stop and back off immediately.

He let me brush his *fetlocks* just as contentedly as he let me brush him everywhere. Occasionally, he'd stomp because a fly was bothering him, but I was never in danger from Joe. I knew that as surely as I knew that Mick would call me fuzz-brain at least once each day.

Mick was very creative in his epithets, but he had a few favorites that he often used. I thought of them as "pet names" for me. Fuzz-brain was one of his top contenders for insults of the day.

I never heard him call Debby anything but Debby. I took a perverse pride in that. He was expending a lot of effort coming up with all those creative insults for me. It took no effort at all to just call someone by their Christian name. I, on the other hand, called Debby every permutation of Big Tooth I could think of. Not to her face. Only in my head. She never spoke to me, at all. She laughed at me a lot, but I can't recall her ever speaking to me. It's possible she just couldn't speak with those giant teeth. It's a wonder her lips could close over those behemoths.

Back to Joe. When I brushed him, if no one was nearby, I would sometimes sing to him. A huge fan of old musicals. I frequently pretended to be Julie Andrews, and knew every song in The Sound of Music. I often brushed Joe while belting out, *Climb Every Mountain.* Sometimes, I brought myself to tears as I screeched into the high notes of the last phrase about finding my dream. Joe often flicked his ears back, and startled. It was a little out of my range, so I had to shriek a bit to hit the note.

One day, I had reached the dramatic climax to the song, and was holding the curry comb to my mouth like a microphone, one arm outstretched the way Julie Andrews did when she was twirling on the mountain top.

Joe's ears flicked, but then stayed back. Silence fell. Then I heard a slow, loud chapping behind me. I didn't need to turn around to know who was there. Joe's ears were a dead giveaway of Mick's presence.

"I didn't think you could sing," he said, as I closed my eyes cringing, "And so I wasn't surprised."

He walked away, singing "till you find your scream," but I never turned around. I leaned against Joe's neck, burying my flaming face in his thick hair. He nibbled at my arm. It might not have been to comfort me…he may have been looking for carrots as I often carried them in my pockets, but it felt like comfort. He stayed like that for a moment, resting his cheek against me.

Why did I care what Mick thought? Why indeed. I can't figure that out even fifty years later. Despite his incredible cruelty, taunting, and dislike of me, I mooned over him. I lay awake at night thinking of his mischievous grin, his sandy hair, his steely blue eyes. I thought of how tomorrow would be different. He would recognize how ugly and deformed Debby was and he would fall in love with me. But it was not to be. Tomorrow came, and instead of endearments, he watched me trip over the pitchfork, stabbing my ankle severely, and grumbled, "Dork."

That pierced ankle was only one of many injuries I sustained at the farm. It could have, and by all rights, should have been much worse. Milly and Burton often disappeared, leaving a barnful of kids and dangerous animals alone. Their level of Benign Neglect teetered on criminal.

One cold day, we were all ice-skating on the little pond in the field where Joe liked to stand. I fell, and stabbed my knee with the back of my ice-skate. It was so incredibly frigid that I don't think I registered any pain. But it felt wet where I had stabbed myself. I was wearing stretchy warm up pants and there was a little hole in the fabric near my knee. I grabbed the hole and stretched it apart so I could look at the scratch. The wetness was blood. Lots of it. And my knee was sliced open in a gaping wound. I almost passed out looking at it.

Burton and Milly were nowhere in sight. I took off my ice-skates and walked the mile home, my knee split open with a good three-inch long, inch-deep sever. When I walked in the door, my mom called down, "Leave your stinky things in the laundry room."

"I think I hurt myself," I called back. She came racing downstairs, looked at my knee, and sped me to the emergency room. I received a passel of stitches. She may have practiced Benign Neglect when all was well, but when one of her brood was injured, she moved with great alacrity. (Look it up if you don't know what it means. I had to.)

In fact, Mom was world-renowned for her ability to sniff out appendicitis. People would bring their loved ones to her. "Bess, is it appendicitis or food poisoning?" Mom would do a few little tests, and then pronounce her verdict. And she was never wrong. Three of my siblings had appendicitis, so she had plenty of practice.

Believe it or not, that ice-skating wound is not the scariest thing that happened to me when Burton and Milly weren't around. All of us kids were hanging out in the barn one day, when Mick came roaring in.

"Zeke's loose!" he bellowed. Now Mick was fearless, but his face was filled with terror.

All of the kids jumped up and looked out into the yard. Zeke, who was a Doberman specifically trained to kill, (or so we'd been told,) came racing toward us. My knees buckled, and I almost fell down. I grabbed at the wall, heart pounding. My muscles went slack, and I froze. Now I understood why people talk about deer in the headlights. That is probably what I looked like.

Fortunately, that was not what happened to Mick. He instantly grabbed little Peeper in his arms and shoved her up the loft ladder.

"Into the loft!" he ordered.

Zeke was fortuitously side-tracked by a chicken. I felt sorry for the chicken, but it afforded us the time to scramble up the ladder into the loft. As we cowered in the loft, peeking out, Mick ordered us all to be silent.

"And don't move," he whispered.

I didn't argue, but I wondered what the big deal was. We were all safely fifteen feet above the floor, with the only access being the vertical wood ladder. Zeke finished dispatching the chicken, and then nose to ground, began running to the barn. As he entered the barn, he sniffed a beeline right to the ladder, and looked up.

We ducked out of sight, but it didn't matter. Zeke's nose knew we were there. And now I understood Mick's frenzied instructions. That Doberman, trained to kill, began to climb the ladder. *Impossible.* Dogs don't climb ladders. Except I was there, and *that* dog was climbing the ladder. There was no other way down, and there was no place to hide. We were all about to meet the same fate as the chicken.

Step by step, Zeke pulled himself up to the next rung. Our only weapons were the hay bales. Mick tried to drop one on Zeke, but he missed. And when Zeke saw Mick, he doubled his efforts. We were goners.

Now Zeke was half way up the ladder, growling and menacing with teeth bared. Then we heard a louder growl. A truck! Burton's truck. He pulled into the yard and instantly assessed the situation. He sprinted into the barn and grabbed Zeke by the back leg, crashing him to the ground. I don't know why Zeke wasn't interested in killing Burton, but Burton alone was safe and able to control him. He grabbed Zeke firmly by the choke collar, and hauled him roughly back to his chain.

"Holy ##@$$%^&&***#!" little Peeper squeaked.

"You got that right," Mick said. I noticed he had planted himself in front of his little sister, and in fact, in front of all of us. Zeke may have killed every one of us, but he'd have had to get through Mick first.

Chapter Eight

The first spring thaw began to melt the snow. As I brushed Joe, I leaned against his warmth, especially on the bitter cold days. He munched hay happily, and took no notice of me. I glanced at his ears. Perked forward and happy, like they usually were with me.

I leaned an arm across his back. He continued munching. I leaned a second arm over his back, watching his ears. They twitched, and he paused briefly, but then resumed his chewing. Emboldened, I lay the weight of my upper torso on his back. He remained unperturbed.

Mick and Debby were in the yard, chipping ice from the water trough and refilling it. Milly sat on a hay bale nearby, cleaning a bridle. She glanced over, and I think we had the same thought simultaneously.

She flicked her braid to her back, and peered at me with a grin.

"Want me to show you how to put on his hackamore?" she asked.

I nodded.

Milly brought me to the tack room and showed me which one was Joe's hackamore amidst the long row of bridles. Once I knew what to look for, it was easy to spot. It was the only one without a bit. She handed it to me, and began pointing out the parts. It was really just like a bridle, except without a bit, and I had already learned to bridle the trail horses. I remembered however, how violently Joe objected to being bridled by Mick. He had tossed his head, and pulled away, even threatened to bite Mick. Mick was brutal, and always won those battles. I was not nearly the experienced horseman Mick was. If there was a battle, I would not win.

As I approached Joe with the hackamore, I said a little prayer. Now I was not at all what you would call religious, but I did think there was some sort of creator of the universe. I wasn't sure who He was, or even if He was a He…but I had a sense that God in some form existed. My prayers back then were usually very brief, and always ended the same way: *Amen, to angels and all.* I didn't want to slight any supernatural being, and since I was unsure of who that all entailed, I thought it best to be all-inclusive.

"Want to go for a ride, Joe?"

He perked his ears toward me, and looked interested. I held the hackamore out to him, as though it were a carrot. He nibbled at it a little, then looked at me.

Carefully, and slowly, I slipped the hackamore up his nose and over his ears. He twitched his ears as I fiddled with his forelock, straightening it so it fell neatly over the brow piece.

"There. You look very nice," I said.

"I'll give you a leg up," Milly said.

Nodding, I unhooked Joe's lead from the wall, and led him out to the riding ring. Mick glanced up as we clip-clopped by.

"Now this I gotta see," he said. Debby looked up and flashed her gargantuan teeth at him. It's a wonder he wasn't blinded in the sun reflecting off all that dental work.

I only allowed myself that brief unkind thought while leading Joe to the ring. My heart was pounding. I knew Joe loved me. Still, he had a whole history of abuse by people on his back, and I was not a good rider. With the exception of 'soft hands', not much else was in my favor. If Joe chose to buck, I would not last a second.

Milly walked beside me. Mick and Debby trailed us, whispering to each other. I was glad I couldn't hear what they were saying. In all likelihood, they weren't complimenting my new sweatpants.

We entered the ring. Mick and Debby climbed onto the top fence rail, smiling and winking at each other. You'd think their perverted delight in my ineptitude would grow old, but it didn't seem to.

Milly cupped her hands and held them out for my knee. Joe was not a big horse, but he was bigger than Skippy. It took me a bit of scrambling and hoisting to finally get my leg over his back. With a deep sigh, I sat straight, settling into the exaggerated sway of his back. I think everyone held their breath. Except Joe.

He glanced at me, turned his head, and nibbled at my boot. Then he nickered, as if to say, "Let's get this show on the road."

"Walk," I said, squeezing my heels gently into his sides. He stepped forward immediately, ears still happily stretched forward. The beauty of a deeply sway-backed horse is that the rider is nestled firmly in the natural saddle. I felt more secure on Joe than even on trusty little Skippy.

Halfway around the ring, I squeezed Joe's sides again.

"Trot."

Joe broke into a trot that was just as teeth-shattering as Skippy's. I was a better rider than when I'd first endured Skippy's trot, but still had trouble keeping my seat on bouncy gaits.

My wildly bobbing ponytails, and less than perfect seat during the trot set Mick off again into peals of laughter.

"At least she's a good rider," he said.

Joe flicked his ears back, at Mick's voice. He snorted.

"Look out now!" Mick called, certain that the bucking was about to commence.

I squeezed Joe's sides, and with my vibrating voice, said, "C-c-canter, Joe."

As terrible as Joe's trot was, his canter was delightful. I no longer feared my teeth were to be crushed into dust. My pony tails streamed behind me, as dear sweet Joe cantered. Passing Mick and Debby with a look of triumph, we circled the ring a second time. Then I slowed Joe to a walk, gently pulling back on the reins. "Hoooo, boy." Joe quietly plodded back towards the gate. Mick and Debby had melted away.

"I wouldn't have believed that if I hadn't seen it," Milly said, "Joe *always* bucks."

Joe shook his head. Not *always*.

"You go ahead and take him on the trail," Milly suggested, smiling at me, a look of tenderness on her face, "He looks like he's having fun." She opened the gate for me and I rode him out. I had not been on the trail since that disastrous day on Skippy. All my riding had been in the ring, when I was learning. Then winter had arrived, and trail rides were over till the spring.

The trail was muddy, with the melting snow, and a little icy in spots where deep ruts had filled with water and then frozen. So most of the way, I kept Joe at a walk. The robins were just beginning to return from their southern vacation spots. Trees were still devoid of buds, but the slightest hint that spring was on its way whispered in the breeze. The cold didn't knife through my wool jacket. The fields were still fallow, and brown. It was not the most spectacular of scenery, even when everything was in bloom. But to me, it could not have been more magnificent. As we walked alone along the empty trail, I sang to Joe. I was not any better at singing than I was at riding, but Joe really did seem to like to listen to me.

I sang the lovely tune titled, "Que sera, sera, whatever will be, will be."

Joe's ears flicked back as he listened then pivoted forward again, as a robin flew by and landed on the fence beside us.

I had done the trail circuit in the cart with Joe, but this was the first time I had ridden it. Joe trotted briefly, but the footing was so uncertain with the icy patches, that I decided it was best just to walk.

When we returned to the barn, it was close to dinner time. I saw Debby in the distance walking back to her home. Mick was in the field with his father, feeding the horses. Milly was breaking open bales in the barn for the boarders.

She glanced up as I stopped in the yard. I slid off of Joe, surprisingly landing on my feet. Lifting the reins over his head, I held his muzzle in my hands. Then I kissed his soft nose, and leaned my face against his.

Milly straightened and rubbed the small of her back. She was not an old woman, as I had initially thought, but farm work was hard, and rough on a body. I led Joe into the barn.

"I'll help you," I said, "As soon as I unbridle Joe."

"Oh you go ahead and brush him," she said, "I think he deserves it, don't you? He can have his dinner inside today."

Pulling off the hackamore, I clipped Joe's lead to his halter. He watched me as I walked into the tack room, hung the hackamore on its nail, and then grabbed a soft brush. Laying the brush on a hay bale near him, I grabbed some sections of a broken bale, and plopped them in front of him.

"How was he on the trail?" Milly asked.

"He was perfect."

"Did he try to run away with you on the way back?"

"No."

She gazed at me as she gathered another handful of hay. After dumping that in a manger, she returned. "You know, Joe is a great cart horse, but he was also a champion barrel racer."

"What's that?" I asked.

"It's one of the classes in a Western Show. Barrels are set up around the ring, and the horse is timed racing around the barrels in a certain pattern as fast as he can go. That's how we met Joe. We saw him in a show barrel racing. He was lightning fast."

I began brushing Joe. He crunched his hay, and Milly still watched me. I had the feeling she expected me to say something, but what was there to say?

"What happened that Joe wouldn't let anyone saddle him anymore?" I asked, in the gaping conversational hole.

"I don't know if we know the whole story," Milly said, "They told us that he got a wasp trapped under the saddle that kept stinging him. That may be true, but when Joe balked at the saddle they beat him. And then when he bucked them off, they whipped him. Joe got meaner, and so did they. Burton saw that happen once, and offered to buy Joe right then and there."

I stopped brushing Joe and looked at Milly.

"Foolhardy thing to do," she added, "We don't have money for a horse that doesn't earn his keep. Joe was never going to be a trail horse. We tried, of course. Hoping that it was just that good-for-nothing owner Joe hated. I guess the abuse made him hate everyone."

I chewed on that thought for a while, feeling sorry for my poor, old horse. Stroking his soft muzzle, my heart ached for all creatures whose nature could be so easily warped by mistreatment.

"And we can't send him on a trail ride without a saddle anyway," Milly said, "No way anyone was ever gonna get a saddle on him again."

Joe had finished his hay, and was looking at me. It almost looked like he was saying, "Is she talking trash about me again?"

"It wasn't really Joe's fault," I said meekly.

"No. No it wasn't."

I glanced outside. Long shadows, low sun. It was time to head home. If only I could just sleep in the loft on those magical days when the spell of Burton's Farm settled like a blanket on my soul. I put the brush away and untied Joe.

"I'll just put him back out in the field before I go," I told her. She nodded and went back to gathering bundles of hay.

"Vicky…wait," she said.

I stopped and turned. Joe nuzzled my back.

"There's an empty standing stall. Until we get a boarder, do you want to keep Joe in there? Then when you finish your chores here you won't have to take the extra time to catch him. It will give you a little more time with him."

I was too shy to say what was in my heart. Had I been a braver child, I would have gushed, *Oh Milly! You are one of the kindest people I know! Underneath all those wrinkles and leathery skin beats a heart of pure compassion!*

"Okay," I said instead, and led Joe to the toasty warm standing stall before jogging home along the busy highway.

Chapter Nine

Spring arrived, but not without taking its sweet time. Joe and I were inseparable. When I was doing chores, if he could be nearby, I always had him with me. While I milked Cindy the goat, from where I'd tied her to the fence, he watched me. As I mucked the stalls, he waited in the barn main room so I could visit him every time I passed by with the tottering wheelbarrow. When the trail rides recommenced, Joe, tied near the other horses, watched as I helped saddle and bridle them. I always took little breaks to nuzzle against him, and slip him a carrot from my pocket. He liked to nibble at my cheek. I think it was his way of giving a horse kiss. Mick watched that behavior and warned me that Joe was tasting me to see if I was worth biting.

"Pretty sad when you taste so bad that the meanest horse on earth won't bite you," he'd say, but his words carried little sting. The meanest horse on earth was rubbing his cheek against mine, and closing his eyes as I whispered to him, "Good horse, Joe."

True to her word, Milly dissuaded Mick from taking Joe as the lead trail horse most of the time. There were still times when he would override her veto, pointing out that the other horses needed to be rested for the back-to-back trails, especially on busy weekends.

Those times tortured me. Despite how gentle Joe was with me, he continued to buck and shy from Mick. This infuriated Mick, more so than before. He seemed to hold it personally against me, and even more angrily, against Joe. If anything, he would spur him more cruelly, race him into a lather more ferociously, and seesaw at his mouth with the reins more brutally.

I did not understand Milly's response to all this. She did little to temper Mick's unkindness to Joe. I could not square that with her compassion towards me, nor her knowledge of Joe's background that had led to his behavior. I guess people are sometimes an incomprehensible mess of contradiction. However, she did try to keep Mick off of Joe, and I was grateful for that.

After a while, Mick himself seemed to tire of Joe. Clearly, Joe was never going to be the docile friend to Mick that he was to me, and Mick lost interest in tormenting me over Joe. I don't know what precipitated the change of heart, but the times between Mick riding Joe stretched into longer periods, until I really was Joe's sole rider.

The first horse show was scheduled for early summer. The farm made money on the horse shows, so they were a big deal, and vital to Burton and Milly's survival. All the workers were allowed any horse they wanted for the show, but they had to pay for the classes. Milly told me I should *for sure* enter Joe in the driving class. She told me with some sheepishness that Mick had requested Joe for the Barrel Race.

During this time, the farm appropriated a new horse. I don't know the whole story, but suspect Burton won him in some sort of bet. He was not the sort of horse that belonged at Burton's Farm. First, he was beautiful. He was sleek, and fit, and young. Secondly, he had the smoothest gaits of any horse that ever lived. I guess I don't know that for certain. However, despite my terrible riding skill, even *I* sat solidly with my bottom glued to his back through all his gaits, including his trot. I didn't jostle at all. It was like riding butter. No horse ever made me look like a better rider than Rockabye did. It was Milly who suggested that I ride Rockabye in the Western Pleasure class. I couldn't ride Joe for two reasons. First, he had to be saddled for that class, and that wasn't happening in this lifetime. Secondly, Joe had a jarring trot and I was not going to do well in any class with my precarious seat and bottom bouncing up and down like a Mexican jumping bean.

So, I started splitting my riding time between Joe and Rockabye. Joe watched me when I saddled Rockabye and led him off to the ring. I don't know what went through Joe's head. Was he jealous? Who can tell with a horse? He did seem to nuzzle me a little more vigorously when I returned, but I don't know if that was a coincidence. I loved Joe in a way I can't begin to describe. But there was no horse more pleasant to ride than Rockabye.

Well, wouldn't you know it, but someone else was interested in Rockabye. Yep, Mastodon Teeth Debby wanted to ride Rockabye in some classes too. Milly told her I had Rockabye for Western Pleasure, but other than that, Debby could have him for the classes she wanted to enter. That meant I had to share practice time on Rockabye with Debby. This was like sharing lunch with a shark. For each time I practiced on Rockabye, Debby got twenty. Maybe she was measuring the ratio of practice time by our respective square inches of teeth. In that case, it was totally fair.

My woes were not over. Milly announced that whoever wanted Rockabye could have him...free. All they had to do was take over paying his board, and he was their horse. Let me be clear. She didn't mean just as long as they worked at the farm. She meant literally, Rockabye would be their horse, till the day they died. Which to a nine-year-old, means forever. (Actually, by then I was ten-years-old, but the same sense of immortality pertained.)

I was just a stupid kid and didn't realize that it is the cost of the upkeep of a horse that breaks people, not the cost of the horse itself. (Unless you are talking about racehorses or champions...but none of Burton's Farm horses came close to that. Not even Rockabye.) I thought this was an offer no one should refuse, especially my parents. Joe belonged to my heart above all else, but no one was offering me Joe for free. Beyond a doubt, the Tooth-full Wonder would be begging her parents for Rockabye too. I had to act quickly. There was no choice but to race home (before Debby) to ask my folks for this impossible-to-pass-up deal. Well, my parents were not as naïve as me. No, we could not afford the upkeep of a horse.

I was not broken-hearted, since my loyalties remained with my beloved Joe. However, I was vindictive, and was not pleased to hear that my nemesis was the new owner of Rockabye. She came to the farm the next day smiling like a Cheshire Cat. Then she announced that her parents had agreed to take over the payments for Rockabye's board. She high-fived Mick, and both of them waited for me to rent my clothes and wail, throwing ashes in the air. I didn't. I was secretly relieved. How could I abandon Joe? Debby agreed to let me ride Rockabye in the Western Pleasure class, mostly because Milly said no deal unless she agreed to that. However, since he was her horse now, all my practice sessions ended.

Life could have been worse. I looked on the bright side. Milly had promoted me to be a trail follower! I was becoming a fairly competent rider on Joe by now, and since Joe was never used for the paying riders, he was always fresh as a trail follower. It was by far my favorite duty at the farm, and spared the older kids for the work I was just too small and weak to accomplish.

This is not to say that my career as a trail follower was not without mishap. I was good at yelling at the riders to pick their horses' heads up when they stopped to munch grass. However, I had no talent at catching runaway horses, especially if the panicked rider was still on them. Mick was exceptionally good at this task. Each time he caught a runaway, and returned to the trail, leading the huffing horse, he muttered at me, "Useless turd."

And I was. Still, he didn't have to point it out. At least not *every* time. Maybe one in ten would have been sufficient to get the point across.

I grew better as I grew older. I'd been at the farm a year as spring morphed into summer and the Horse Show was upon us!

All of us workers at the farm were responsible for helping out at the horse show, except of course during the classes we entered. I cannot remember if anyone in my family showed up for my first horse show. They might have. I just don't remember. Since I can't find any pictures of the momentous event, I suspect I didn't even tell them about it.

In fact, the horse show itself is a bit of a blur. I do remember some very brief snippets from that day. There were two horses in the driving class, which means I was guaranteed at least a second place ribbon. Joe was magnificent. He did everything perfectly, winning second place. Milly reminded me that I didn't ever need to tell anyone that there were only two horses in the event. She assured me I would have won second place if there had been twenty horses! I never pressed her on how she knew that.

Then came my Western Pleasure Class on Rockabye. I hadn't ridden Rockabye in a month because …well, you know why. We don't need to pick at wounds. Anyway, it was like stealing candy from a baby. Rockabye was that good. I didn't need to do a single thing but sit there. As soon as the announcer said, "Trot," Rockabye trotted. As soon as he said, "Canter," Rockabye cantered. I have no doubt that if he had said, "Make a Crème Brulee," Rockabye would have made a Crème Brulee.

I won first place. And there was more than one horse. It was a huge class, in fact. If I had entered ten classes with Rockabye, I would have had ten blue ribbons. However, more pride swelled my little head over my second place ribbon. That one had required effort.

Handing the reins of the amazing Rockabye off to Tremendous-Teeth signaled the end of my career as a prize-winning rider. I crept back into the barn to the standing stall where Joe was taking a little nap. He opened his dreamy eyes as I slipped in beside him.

"Hi buddy," I whispered, stroking his soft muzzle.

He blew a blast of hot air into my palms, and closed his eyes again as I rubbed behind his ears.

His day was not over. He still had the Barrel Racing class with Mick. I was a mess over that, but I had no control over Mick. While I was brushing Joe, Mick came to his stall.

"I need Joe for my class," he said.

I turned and looked at Mick. For the first moment in my complete adoration of the unattainable Mick, I felt a tinge of hatred.

"Don't hurt him, Mick," I said. I looked straight at him. Mick looked back at me, his face purpling like he was about to explode. Instead, he just closed his mouth. His mouth contorted a few times, as though he were actually considering his words. "What do you see in this horse?" he finally said.

Everything you don't see.

I didn't answer. I didn't know the Bible yet, but maybe it had something to do with casting pearls before swine. Backing Joe out of the stall, I took the hackamore from Mick.

"I'll get him ready for you," I said.

Joe's ears were back, and he was sidestepping in agitation.

"Ho, boy," I said, petting his neck, while following Mick out to the yard. I put the hackamore on Joe, and then Mick (surprisingly) told me I could walk Joe to the ring and wait with him. The Barrel Races had already begun. I was surprised to see Joe's ears flick forward, and his expression change from fear to attentiveness. He watched the horses racing around the barrels with a look that I can only describe as eager.

"I'm up," Mick said.

I handed him Joe's reins, and he catapulted onto Joe's back. Joe sidestepped and tossed his head, but didn't buck. His ears were tipped forward, and he was looking at the barrels with full concentration. Mick's name was announced, and Joe pranced to the start line. The announcer said, "Go!"

Like a shot, Joe was off. If you have ever watched Barrel Racing, you know how athletic those horses are. Joe came so close to the barrels that he grazed them as he wheeled around them. At times, it didn't seem like he could possibly remain upright with the severe angle he cut around the barrel. He looped in a cloverleaf pattern around three barrels, and then Mick was digging his heels in him and yelling, "Haaaaaa!" I had never seen Joe gallop as fast as he did down the homestretch, from the last barrel to the finish line.

Joe won by several seconds. He left the competition in the dust. He was snorting and huffing as Mick wheeled him to a stop and leaped off his back. Debby was there to hug him. I was there to take Joe's reins.

Mick glanced at me, as I grabbed the reins.

For a moment, I thought he was going to thank me, but then, his expression changed, and he was locked in an embrace with Metal Mouth.

Joe's sides were heaving. I led him away from the crowded ring, and walked him for a long time up and down the trail, till his breathing slowed. There was a sparkle in his eye that I hadn't seen before.

"Did you have fun?" I asked him.

Joe nickered and muzzled at my pocket. As usual, I had a carrot, and of course, he knew it.

Chapter Ten

The days and months of summer passed way too quickly. Those were idyllic times at the farm. I left my house by 9 a.m. each morning and didn't return till dinnertime. Every day. My parents sometimes wondered aloud if they had left their daughter Vicky in Memphis because they hadn't seen hide nor hair of her since moving to Illinois.

The farm workers were rewarded with unlimited pop, as well as horse riding privileges. My favorite was orange soda. Since I don't recall ever going home for lunch, I guess my lunch was orange soda all summer long. I drank it by the gallons on those hot summer days. Sometimes after a trail ride, Mick would sit with me in the tack room where the soda machine was. We would guzzle our pop, while perched on hay bales. He made a great show of heaving enormous burps, which always made me giggle.

I was becoming a good rider veering into my 11th birthday. I rode every day of the summer. Burton's Farm was very popular for trail rides, and so I was doing several trail rides a day. Joe was completely dependable. Since the trails were mostly walked, with the brief spurt of trotting, he never grew tired. I was a small, light-framed little girl and so hardly heavy on his back. Once in a while, I was even successful stopping a runaway horse and returning him to the trail. Again, it was less my skill than the skill of my horse. Joe hated other horses, and was not nice to them at all. Since I was at the end of the line, if a trail horse decided he wanted to turn back to the barn, he had to get past Joe.

Well Joe would have none of that. If he saw the horse fall out of line and start heading towards him, Joe would show his teeth, snort, and leap at the horse. That was quite often all that was necessary.

Mick stopped calling me *useless turd,* though he didn't replace it with encouraging commendations. He just didn't talk to me much at all. It could be that he had grown weary of my muteness in his presence. It's not like I was a sparkling conversationalist and a joy to chat with. Except with Joe. I told Joe everything. I talked non-stop when Joe and I were alone.

"Joe, have you ever wondered why there are mosquitoes? I can't come up with a single good reason." Joe watched me, but didn't answer. "While we are on the subject of whys, why am I so afraid to talk to people? I can think of a million things to say when no one is around. You'd think I had my tongue cut out the way I lose the power of speech around everyone but you."

Joe knew everything there was to know about me. To his credit, he wasn't a gossipy horse, and what happened with Joe, stayed with Joe.

Except when Mick overheard me. That unfortunately happened too often for my taste. Then he resumed his taunting while I blushed and pretended not to hear him.

"You wish you could marry Robin, rather than Batman?!" Mick shrieked. I don't think he needed to broadcast that secret to the entire farm. Sometimes I think he purposely snuck up on me and Joe to eavesdrop.

The fall snatched the glorious summer from my grasp, and school resumed. I'm afraid I let slip to Joe one day that I had been selected for the solo in our 6th grade choir concert. Joe thought that was no surprise, since the best I ever sang was when I sang to him. There's no doubt Joe enjoyed my singing. However, after I was selected to be the soloist, the practice sessions commenced. I was so nervous during those times, that the choir director revoked my solo. I may have shed a few tears telling Joe about that.

"You're lucky she did," said the eavesdropping Mick, "Or you would have emptied the auditorium."

Joe snapped back his ears at Mick's voice, as he always did. He looked like he was getting ready to kick him, but I soothed him. "It's ok, Joe, he's just jealous."

Mick swirled around. Had I said that out loud?

"She speaks," he said, in surprise.

I guess I had.

Sixth grade had other unexpected joys however to make up for the singing disappointment. We were assigned a speech topic. Now not surprisingly, this mortified me. Shy, mousy, little me could not imagine getting up in front of the entire 6th grade class. There is just no way I could do that. The assigned topic was "How to Do Something." We could choose to teach about how to do anything we wanted. How about *how to die from a heart attack because of being forced to give a speech in front of the entire 6th grade class?* That one at least I was pretty sure I could do.

I went home that day in a tizzy. The fright was already filling my soul, and my speech was still three weeks away. I grabbed some apple slices and headed to the farm after school. The weather was pleasant, so it was not a tragedy that Joe had lost his standing stall to a new boarder. I called to him, and he came cantering across the field.

"Wait till you hear what I have to do," I told Joe, while haltering him and then leading him into the barn. I walked him over to the fence where Cindy the goat waited for me. Tying Joe to the fence, I grabbed the milk bucket and began automatically milking Cindy. I didn't even need to think about milking any more. My hands knew what to do while my mind wandered.

"I have to teach the class how to do something. What do I know how to do that I can teach? How can I talk in front of the class even if I could teach them something?"

I thought of one of the girls, Nikki, who had bragged that she was going to teach the class how to ride an elephant. It never occurred to me that Nikki might have trouble procuring an elephant. I was exceptionally gullible, and just assumed that was the caliber of talks I was up against.

Joe listened, nodding his head ever so slightly. He watched the milk hiss into the pail as the barn cats gathered around. I aimed a stream into a calico's mouth. My aim had really improved. It went spot on into the cat's gaping mouth.

"Wait!" I said, with a sudden inspiration.

Joe startled, and tossed his head.

"I can teach the class how to milk a goat!" Thus, the idea was born. First, I cleared it with Milly. She approved the idea, but said I would have to find a way to get the goat to my school and back.

My mom was totally with me on the idea. We had a VW microbus, so we would have plenty of room for Cindy. We would just line the van floor with newspaper since Cindy, for all her wonderful attributes, was not house-trained.

Next hurdle was to clear it with the teacher, but to keep it secret from the class. I wanted it to be a surprise. The teacher loved the idea but told me she had to check with the principal.

Get this. Not only did the principal say this sounded like a fabulous idea, but we would do it in the large entry way of the school, and he would invite all the 6th grade classes. Gulp. Shy little me was going to milk a goat in front of the entire Chazak, Illinois 6th grade population.

Fortunately, I knew my subject. I didn't even have to write the speech. Although nervous, I was also excited. Unlike the debacle with my singing solo, no one was going to snatch this away from me.

The day of the speech I was given the morning off from school to go with my mom to get the goat. It was arranged that the principal would gather all the classes and arrange the kids in a ring around the center of the entryway. Afterwards I would arrive with Cindy. We wanted Cindy to have as little time as necessary at the school so she wouldn't be spooked.

Cindy hopped right into the van, and I sat in the back with her, stroking her neck. She bleated a few times, but mostly took it all in stride. When we arrived at the school, I led Cindy up the walkway and through the entry door. I almost fainted looking at the crowd, but Cindy butted me, and the crowd started laughing and clapping. Some were cheering.

"Vicky brought a goat!!"

"This is great!"

"What's she going to do with the goat?"

The crowd quieted in expectation and I was consumed with something I rarely felt: *confidence.*

"Today I'm going to teach you how to milk a goat."

The kids cheered. The teacher smiled broadly. Even the principal was smiling. Lots of other teachers were there too and they were all laughing. Not *at* me. (for once.) *With* me, in delight.

I explained the process, and then demonstrated. The crowd watched breathlessly. It was not at all hard. I don't think I was the slightest bit scared, once I got going. Cindy was perfect too. She did poop a little but we had been prepared. The teacher had covered the entryway floor with newspaper.

Then I asked if anyone would like to try. Several hands went up. I helped each volunteer, the same way Milly had helped me. You can't believe how good it felt to see their faces when milk spurted successfully into the pail.

When it was over, I got a huge round of applause. Cindy chewed her cud, and followed me back out to the van. She hopped in, flicking her tail back and forth, and we drove back to the farm.

"That was wonderful," said Mom.

Yes, it was. And the best part is that it was by far the best speech of the class. (The teacher told me so, and gave me an A$^+$) Incidentally, Nikki did NOT show up with an elephant. She did a speech on how to make a paper airplane.

Chapter Eleven

My baby sister, Holly, was born that year. I guess I haven't mentioned much about my family. It might be a good idea to pause here and tell you a little about them. My family was…different…and helps to explain a whole lot about me. I had an older sister, Wendy, who I hated throughout my childhood. It wasn't really Wendy's fault. Wendy was really smart, really coordinated, and really out-going. That's a lot of *reallys*…but it was really true. All the teachers loved Wendy. Wendy set the standard for all four siblings to follow in her wake. She was just fourteen months older than me, so all the teachers would have Wendy the first year, and then me the following year. Expectations were high when I came along to their classroom.

Let me give you an example of what I was up against. In third grade, we had the same teacher, and we had the same assignment. A research paper. We were both in some accelerated program, but trust me, Wendy was more accelerated than I. Her third grade research paper was on "The Brain." Yes. I know. She did such a stupendous job of researching the brain that college students were invited to hear her presentation. No, I am not kidding. That was the act I was privileged to follow.

"Oh," the grinning teacher said on the first day of class, "You're Wendy's sister!"

That was probably the last time she grinned at me. In contrast to Wendy's college level project on the brain, my third grade research paper was titled, "The Care and Feeding of the Black-Capped Chickadee." I know you think I am lying but it is God's truth. To say I was a disappointment to the third grade teacher would be a gross understatement. And incidentally, no college students were banging on my door begging *me* to read my research paper on the care and feeding of black-capped chickadees to them.

After me, two years later arrived the sole boy, John. John was an underachiever. He didn't hit his stride till college, when he shocked us all. I think my parents knew he was brilliant but I don't think I did. The only strong memory I have of John in my early childhood was of him leaning his face into my pet rabbit's cage and the bunny taking an oval chunk out of his nose. I also remember him setting off model rockets that arced in gleaming majesty far above us. That was spectacular. He does something similar now in his illustrious career.

Fourth was my sister Amy, three years younger than me. We called her "the grudge collector." She was, but I was very close to Amy. I am not sure why. She turned into a fantastic adult and left her grudge collecting days behind. Even she would admit she was a rather critical and unhappy child, collecting slights and nursing them while plotting terrible revenges.

She hated baby Holly as much as I hated Wendy. Part of that was due to the fact that poor Amy had to sleep in the same room as howling baby Holly. When baby Holly woke Amy up one too many times, Amy bit her elbow. That made baby Holly howl louder, and Mom screeched into the room. Amy denied any knowledge of the cause of Holly's wailing. She was sneaky like that.

The year Holly was born, I invited Amy to the farm with me. Amy didn't go nearly as often as I went, but she liked the farm and I have some very good memories of her time there with me.

The final addition to the family, baby Holly, was born when I was eleven-years-old. That was enough for my mom, who initially wanted twelve kids. I don't know which one of us changed her mind. She stopped at five, and any one of us could have been justifiably blamed.

Anyway, Amy started coming to the farm when she was about eight. She learned to ride on a little pony who was perhaps even smaller than Skippy. The pony, Nipper, only had one eye. I am not sure exactly at what point he lost the eye, but it was in the time period that we worked at the farm. I do know he'd gouged the eye out on a stick, and the vet sewed the flap closed where his eyeball had been. Nipper didn't seem to miss it.

I was responsible for teaching Amy to ride. I gave her a knee up, like Milly used to do for me, and she lay on her stomach, stuck like a sack of potatoes across Nipper's back. In an effort to help push her right leg over his back, I ended up shoving her clear off to the other side and onto the hard ground.

She got up and we tried again. Eventually, we got her on little Nipper. That's all I remember. Apparently, Amy learned to ride Nipper, because she still recalls that we quickly graduated her to a larger horse.

She got on the horse, who decided he wasn't interested in Amy riding him. He cantered away, with Amy clinging to his back, jumped the pasture fence and thundered off. At some point, Amy fell off but I don't exactly remember that part. She returned to one-eyed Nipper as her riding steed.

The best Amy story involved that no-man's land of mud in between the pasture and the back barn door. Amy and I were responsible that day to bring in the trail horses. I had already successfully navigated the mud, and my horse was tied and ready to be saddled. I went out to get another horse, and Amy was leading a giant palomino in. When the horse came to the mud, he stopped. He just refused to move forward. Amy tugged on his lead, but she was a tiny little eight-year-old pipsqueak. No way was she going to out-muscle the giant horse.

We shouted some instructions, to no avail. Then someone suggested, *Smack his nose!* It might've been me. I don't recall who said it but I can still hear the words in my mind. It seemed like great advice at the time.

So, Amy did. She smacked the palomino's nose. Without pause, the horse slammed his enormous hoof into the center of Amy's back. She went down like the Titanic, face down into the oozy mud. The mud closed over her, and the horse walked right across her, stepping directly on her back, and into the barn. I thought we'd have to dig to China to recover Amy.

The deep mud probably saved her life. We scurried to unwedge her from the gunk. She was covered head to toe in smelly, black mud and manure. But she was alive, and that was a miracle. Not only alive, but unhurt.

Mom's Benign Neglect saved our future at the farm after that. I don't think she ever knew about Amy's trampling. We were pretty sneaky. We cleaned her up and washed the clothes without Mom's knowledge. This was no small feat to pull off, even with Mom's Benign Neglect. I mean, Amy was covered in thick black mud. In her hair, her ears, and under her nails. Her clothes were caked with it. How could we get her in the bathtub without Mom noticing us sneaking by? We didn't have to be as stealthy as kids who had more nosey parents. Still, it was a daunting task.

First problem after getting Amy safely hidden in the tub. How could I wash the clothes when I had never, not even once, used the washing machine? I decided not to waste too much worry time on that part of the delicate operation. How hard could it be?

I just threw out her socks. They were too nasty to even consider washing. The rest of the stuff, I dumped in the scrub sink, having a sixth sense about putting three or four pounds of manure mud in Mom's washer. The scrub sink quickly clogged. No problem! I filled a nearby bucket with the slop and snuck outside with it. After dumping that, and rinsing the clothes a few times, I tossed them in the washer, put in three cups of detergent, which seemed reasonable at the time, and started it. That turned out to be a mistake. Mom came running.

"Why is the washer going?" she cried. Benign Neglect only extended to children, not to household appliances.

"I started the wash. You know how stinky my clothes get."

Now unfortunately, I'd neglected to notice I was still wearing my stinky clothes, so it didn't have the ring of truth it might have otherwise had.

Mom raised an eyebrow, and pursed her lips. That's when I realized my error, because her nose twitched too. I knew she was smelling my dirty clothes.

"I just washed Amy's," I added quickly, "She fell in the mud."

Bingo! Didn't even have to lie!

Mom's forehead wrinkled. She knew something was up, but of all her kids, I was the most helpful one. Least ways, that's my recollection. She knew better than to doubt her sensitive little girl who out of the goodness of her heart, was doing the laundry.

"Where's Amy?" she asked.

She was showing an uncommon amount of interest in her brood suddenly, and her eyes fell on the drops of manure on the floor.

"She's in the bath." I followed Mom up to the bathroom. I hoped Amy had the wherewithal to keep her mouth shut about what precipitated her fall in the mud.

"Are you okay, Amy? I heard you fell."

Amy glanced at me, peering around Mom. The water was brown, but that was to be expected. I made shushing motions with my finger to lips.

"Yep. Just getting cleaned up."

Mom looked at both of us, but we affected our angelic faces. With a sigh, she turned and left.

"Good job," I whispered to Amy. She turned to let the dirty water out and I gasped when I saw her back.

I'd thought there was no evidence of the crime…and except for one teensy weensy thing, there wasn't. Amy had a perfect hoof-shaped bruise in the middle of her back. I suppose it is possible Mom knew about the whole thing, and just figured kids would be kids. That would fit in with her philosophy on child rearing. Still, I urged Amy to keep her back *incognito* around Mom. Fortunately, Mom was sidetracked by an excess of bubbles leaking into the living room. I learned an important house-keeping lesson that day. One cup of detergent is sufficient.

This was not our only ill-conceived adventure. Since I had become an expert cart driver with Joe, I concocted the crazy idea that my expertise applied to all animals. Amy and I got the brilliant idea that it would be fun to attach a sled to our dog and have her pull baby Holly around. Our dog was a "slow-spotted" sweet Dalmatian, named Lady. Her spots didn't come in till she was well past the age when they should have appeared. She slowly developed spots over the years. She was a plump, good-natured little thing. There was an early snowfall and we were in charge of keeping baby Holly entertained. Since I had an excellent knowledge of harnesses and how to attach carts to them, I used ropes and leashes to rig a harness for Lady. We had a toboggan that would be perfect for the sleigh. After attaching the sleigh to Lady, we put baby Holly in it for a nice winter wonderland jaunt.

Well, as soon as Lady stepped forward and felt the unfamiliar and rather terrifying tug of the sleigh behind her, she freaked. She took off at a surprisingly fast run, with baby Holly bouncing around, likely not enjoying the winter wonderland jaunt as much as we had intended.

Now remember, we lived next to the busy highway, and of course, that was the direction that the frenzied dog headed. We ran as fast as we could, with a lot of yelling and leaping. Baby Holly tumbled off and somehow, after some squealing brakes and angry car horns, Lady looped back to us and we caught her.

We calmed baby Holly as best we could and lied about why she was crying when we returned her to my mother. Again, the wrinkled forehead, and twitching nose, as though she could smell out an untruth. With a clenched jaw, she took baby Holly from us, and Amy and I breathed a sigh of relief.

Now, I haven't mentioned my dad at all. Dad is so unique that he needs at least some explanation. My mom met dad when they worked on the college newspaper together. She said she noticed him because he brought his own typewriter to the newspaper office each day. Mind you, there were plenty of typewriters provided, but Dad had his own special one.

Dad was possibly the first man on earth to wear spandex. He was an avid bicyclist, and when spandex was first invented, Dad got himself a black and orange striped spandex bike outfit. Dad was a jolly, rotund man, so he looked a lot like a bumblebee in that outfit. I was mortified. I knew that other people saw the round spandexed bumble bee on his recumbent bicycle and knew it was my father. And yes. Recumbent bicycle. As if the spandex wasn't humiliating enough, he had one of the first bicycles that stretch out just a few inches from the ground. The rider leans back on a comfy seat with a high cushioned seat back, and reaches up to handlebars which are level with his head. He looked like Mickey Mouse on a Harley Davidson. (Mickey Mouse dressed like a fat Bumblebee.) Yes. Horror and shame filled me whenever Dad put on his spandex. There was no doubt I would hear about it at school on Monday. The only blessing is that Mick never saw my Dad since Dad never came to Burton's Farm.

Unlike Amy, Wendy didn't get my attraction to the farm at all. In general, Wendy didn't quite get me, and took almost as much delight as Mick did in heaping verbal abuse on me. However, she reaped as much abuse from me as she dished out. She was quick to point out what a total uncoordinated klutz I was, but I had one distinct advantage over her. I didn't bite my nails. So they were very useful weapons. Wendy was stronger, bigger, and more coordinated, but she was a nail-biter. She had no sharp weapons and had to rely on brute strength. On the other hand, I strafed her with knife-like fingers all the time. When she complained, and Mom stormed into our room to find out why we were both bawling, I blamed Wendy. I often got away with it, till Wendy began imploring Mom to check under my fingernails for the forensic evidence of my crimes.

On the plus side, almost every night I nagged Wendy to tell me a story. After how mean I was to her, I don't know why she complied, but she did. She may have reminded me that I smelled like horse poop, but she told me wonderful stories, though I fell asleep before most of them ended. Unlike Mick, she had that balance of her treatment of me. Mick could learn a thing or two about beginning all interactions with a positive before ripping headlong into the negative.

So of all my siblings, Amy was my only farm companion. She was in complete agreement of my love affair with horses, but she totally couldn't understand my adoration of Mick. She saw how mean he was to me, now and then tempered with total indifference. Still, as we walked together to the farm along the busy highway, I babbled on and on about all the things Mick could do and how wonderful he was. She never asked why on earth I wasted my love on someone who so clearly despised me.

It is strange. I can clearly picture Burton, Milly, Peeper, Cindy, Zeke, and of course Joe. I can even picture Debby, who I hated with all my heart. But the boy I was head over heels (inexplicably) in love with…I cannot conjure up the slightest image of him. I *think* he had blondish hair. I *think* he had bluish eyes. I *think* he was muscular though of lanky build. But I don't know for sure.

Was it some abstract idea of Mick that I loved so much? Was it the very fact that he despised me that made me try so hard to change his mind? Why would I be able to picture visually so many details of the barn -- the stalls, the sheds, the fields -- but not Mick?

I hated how he rode Joe, though on one level, I think he thought it was the only way to make the useless horse useful to the farm. He may have saved Joe's life, since the farm could hardly afford to keep a horse that didn't bring in some sort of income. By making Joe at least marginally useful as Mick's trail guide horse, he may have tipped the precarious balance in Joe's favor.

Chapter Twelve

The following summer, I was old enough and accomplished enough that Milly made a new stunning offer. I could be a trail leader.

Mick raised his eyebrows, but didn't say anything. As we grew older, he seemed to be a little less nasty. He was still dating Debby, who did get her braces off at some point in my years at the farm. It was probably around this time. Her teeth were still enormous, but at least now there wasn't a ton of steel for her poor lips to contend with as well. Don't get me wrong. I didn't feel sorry for her.

At any rate, with Milly's pronouncement, I felt a swell of pride and joy. If Milly thought I was good enough to lead the trail, I must be at least a decent horsewoman. She threw almost *anyone* at the back as a trail follower, as you have seen, but she was much more discerning in her choice of trail leaders.

I knew I was a favorite. I was a very hard worker who actually enjoyed all the work, even mucking the stalls. Once I got through the year or so of caked manure, maintaining the stalls was not nearly as difficult. I only have clear memories of keeping one or two stalls clean, so I think we were probably assigned a few specific stalls we were responsible for. I always did everything Milly asked. Every new thing she taught me was met with delight and gratitude. I imagine Milly enjoyed being appreciated. How compassionate she was, letting a skinny, frightened, clueless nine-year-old have entrée to her wonderful world. Any way about it, Milly bent over backwards to watch over me and hand me incredible gifts, such as offering to let me be a trail guide!

I was terribly excited about leading a trail, but also a little terrified. I was only twelve... much younger than the adults I would be responsible for. Nonetheless, no one ever challenged my authority or treated me unkindly. Amazing.

The day I was to lead my first trail ride started off just dandy. It was a beautiful fall day, sunny, and clear. The trail was not muddy, and the horses were all feeling relatively perky...as perky as they *ever* felt. Remember, most of these horses were at least thirty years old, and perky was not a word easily applied to any of them. Joe, who was in his late twenties, was a spring chicken compared to most of them. Just to be clear, the average life span of a horse is 25-33 years. Some ponies last into their later thirties, but every horse there was a step away from the Pearly Gates. Burton and Milly could not afford young horses. Most trail riders are totally ignorant about riding, so all they want is the experience of being on a horse that can walk. Burton's horses could do that, but not a whole lot else. That was, in general, a good thing given the lack of experience most trail riders had.

There was one horse besides Rockabye that was an exception. Again, I don't know the story behind that horse, and why Burton's Farm had a three-year-old horse among the geriatrics. Her name was Witch, and from what I had seen, she had earned the name. She was "green-broke" which basically meant she was barely ride-able. She was the most skittery, crazy horse I'd ever seen, but then all I really had to compare her to were the equine senior citizens used as trail horses. Mostly, she was left to herself. I don't know what Burton planned to do with her. No one ever rode her, and the few times someone did, they ended up with some injury. I don't think she was mean, but she shied at everything, and her movements were so unexpected that no one could stay on – not even Mick.

Back to my first trail leading. I whistled for Joe, and as soon as he saw me, he came cantering over to me. It was always a thrill to see how eagerly he greeted me. I don't know if it was because he recognized a fellow misfit, or if he just liked the carrots in my pocket. Whatever the reason, he wanted to be with me.

"We have a very special treat today," I told him, snapping the lead on his halter, "Today, we will lead a trail."

He threw his head up and down, as though he thought that was a fine idea. Since I had found him far down the back pasture, I clambered up onto his back. He never used a bit anyway, and a halter and lead was pretty effective for a neck-reining horse. Just in case some of you are not fortunate enough to have ever ridden a horse, I better explain neck-reining. Neck-reining is using the reins' pressure on the horse's neck to indicate the direction he should go. There are two types of riding – English and Western. In English riding, one holds the reins in two hands, and pulls the

106

reins on the same side one wants the horse to turn. In Western riding, which is what we did at Burton's Farm, one uses one hand and brings the reins across the neck on the opposite side one wants to turn. I have always preferred Western riding, maybe because that is how I learned to ride.

Joe was a wonderful neck-reiner. It took almost no tugging from me for him to turn quickly the way I wanted him to go. With the halter lead, I could only neck rein in one direction, but I would shift my weight and pull on his mane to get him to go the other direction if needed. He always went where I wanted him to go. It was like he could read my mind. We had an uncanny connection. Besides, he knew where the barn was, and he knew that when I brought him in the barn, he always got some grain, carrots, and a wonderful brushing. So it may not have been uncanny at all, but obvious where we were headed and why it behooved him to not dawdle.

While we're talking about it, don't gloss over the fact that without any kind of mounting block, I was able to climb aboard Joe. There were no mounting blocks in the middle of the pasture. To ride Joe to the barn from the field, I had to learn how to mount unassisted. I had come a long way since the first embarrassing need to use the baby block to mount. I wasn't nearly as acrobatic or impressive as Mick, but I could now get on Joe without anyone's help.

Once atop him, I leaned forward and threw my arms around his neck.

"Oh Joe! Just think of it. We are going to lead a trail!"

He flicked his ears back, listening to me, then trotted happily to the barn. We managed to make it safely through the mud pit without incident and rode into the barn. Mick was not there that day, which is probably why Milly had told me I would lead a trail ride. I don't know where Mick was, but I was glad my virgin attempt at trail guiding would not take place under his condemning eyes.

I brushed Joe with special care. For our first time leading a trail, we needed to be particularly sparkling. The other workers were getting the trail horses ready. Debby was not helping. Since she now owned her own horse, she didn't need to do any farm work. I don't recall her doing anything but ride Rockabye once she was his owner, and of course, hang out with Mick. But I'm not complaining. I loved the farm work. She was missing out, as far as I was concerned.

The trail riders gathered, and were helped onto their horses. I led Joe out to the yard, and impressed everyone by leaping agilely upon his back. Okay, not really, but I didn't make anyone ask for a refund either, and that was a bonus. The workers lined up the riders behind me, told them to follow me, and we were off. One of the teens was the follower, on a somewhat skittish pony.

As we plodded along, the trail horses did what they always did. Every chance they got, they stopped to munch grass, or snatch leaves off of branches which lined the trail edges. I was constantly turning around, and urging them to pull up their horse's head, or kick their horses' sides so they would move on from their snack. It is hard not to be disgusted by the incompetence of people who have never been on a horse.

I was annoyed. It was normally the follower's duty to urge the riders to keep moving, but the teen follower was having a little trouble with the skittish pony.

"Kick him, and he will stop eating the tree," I urged one of the riders.

"I did. He won't go."

"He will if you kick him hard enough."

"I don't want to hurt him."

I don't want to hurt you, but I will…so help me, God.

"Try pulling on the reins so he will bring his head up, and then kick him."

"I did try that."

No, you didn't. I have been watching you the whole time and you are just sitting there like a lump of playdoh letting the horse do whatever he wants.

"He seems really hungry. Are you sure he gets enough to eat at that farm?"

"Yes ma'am, he's just a pig. Kick him a little harder."

The adult made a few ineffectual tugs at the reins, and kicked the horse's sides so lightly that all she disturbed was a bit of dust.

With a sigh, I stopped the others, and went back to the horse. I whacked him on his butt and his head sprung up. He glared at me, but grudgingly moved forward. I trotted back to the front of the trail.

Joe was a wonderful guide horse. He remained calm, and quiet, despite the numerous times, I swiveled around, laid one hand on his rump, and screamed instructions. I now began to understand some of Mick's disdain. People are idiots. They just are. It pains me to say this, but the truth is the truth. I mean, how hard was it to figure out that when a horse drops his head to eat grass, all you have to do is pull on the reins, and he will pick his head up? It is not rocket science, people.

Murderous thoughts roared through my head, but to my credit, I kept most of them to myself. I think Joe sensed my growing annoyance, however. Joe knew me better than anyone by now. I was never anything but gentle and kind with him. I think he sensed there was a growing fury within me that he didn't recognize. At least not in me. I think he sensed it in Mick, and it is why he never calmed under Mick's hands.

We had stopped for the ten-thousandth time because of one particular woman and her greedy horse, who quickly figured out that his rider was not going to prevent him from grazing the entire hour of the trail ride. Other riders were becoming annoyed as well. Finally, in exasperation, I rode back to the horse and smacked him with my whip. The trail leaders always were given a whip. I knew I would never use it on Joe, but I even surprised myself when I used it on Fatso, grazing one time too many.

The horse bolted forward, though settled almost immediately back into a walk. However, an unfortunate chain reaction was initiated. The follower's pony, who was already antsy, saw the horse bolt out of the corner of his eye, and shied. With his eyes ringed in terror, not quite knowing the source of the scuffling nearby, he took off at a gallop. The teen, somehow, clung to him, having successfully gathered a handful of his mane.

The pony rocketed past the line-up of sleepy horses. Coming from behind like that, he startled all of them. As he galloped ahead, those old nags of one accord, took off after him. Horses are herd animals, and if one of them is running, they figure there is a reason, and they all should be running.

It would be no exaggeration to say I had lost control of my trail group. Even my normally responsive Joe thundered off after the crazed pony. The only saving grace was that we were far enough out of sight of the barn that Milly never saw any of it.

The horses galloped like nobody's business for a good five minutes. They had covered half the trail ride in no time. I don't remember a single trail rider falling off, which proves beyond a shadow of a doubt that there is a God.

Finally, the instigator slowed, and with heaving sides stopped. The rest of the gang had reached the limit of their endurance as well, and they all huffed and puffed to a halt as well.

I smiled weakly at them all, as we stood there. All our horses' heads were hanging, with breath erupting in spurts.

"Normally they only let us walk on these trail rides," observed one rider.

"Can we do that again?" asked one of the older children. I noticed his parents looked a little green.

"No, we only allow one gallop on the trail rides," I squeaked.

"I'm surprised it's allowed at all," another said, "Does anyone ever fall off?"

I didn't answer. I was anticipating what the crowd would be reporting to Milly when we got back to the barn. The trail riders lined up behind me again as we embarked on the last half of our ride at a plodding walk. The pony's rider had slipped off of her wild pony, and was leading him. I think she had had enough excitement for the day.

I would have enjoyed the trail ride a whole lot more if I wasn't so worried about what I would tell Milly. I had never lied to her, but I didn't see how I could admit what had happened. And surely one of the trail riders would spill the beans.

"I don't always let the trail riders gallop," I ventured.

"Oh?" said one of them.

"No, only when they seem like they are really good riders and I think they will stay on."

The riders all puffed up a bit.

"It's not always *strictly* allowed so I kind of keep it quiet," I continued, "I don't want the riders to get in trouble."

"If we do this again, we will ask for you!" one rider said.

I grinned weakly. If I was ever allowed to lead another trail, I'd be a little less snotty and condescending.

When we arrived back at the barn, Milly looked at me curiously.

"Back so soon?"

I took a deep breath.

"She let us go fast," the kid said.

No one else said a word. Fast could mean many things. I knew Milly might think fast meant trot. A trot is very fast to a novice rider. She noticed the teen leading the prancing pony.

"Why are you walking?"

"My pony seemed a little nervous," she said.

Again, Milly cocked her head, and looked at us with some perplexity. She shrugged her shoulders and let it go. I know she was too savvy not to have suspected something was amiss. However, I had returned with every rider and horse intact, no one was complaining, and she had the money safely stowed in the lock box. In her world, that was a successful trail ride. She didn't need to hear the details, and she sure wasn't   going   to   hear   them   from   me.

Chapter Thirteen

The only other serious injury I incurred at the farm happened on another trail ride. As Witch had shown us, shying horses are the nemesis of controlled rides. The few times anyone tried to ride her, she shied continually, dumping riders like dandruff. She became completely useless as a trail horse. I don't recall Joe ever shying while I rode him, except once. But for that one exception, he was unfailingly careful with me, as though I were precious cargo. Don't worry. We'll get to that story soon.

There is no doubt Joe loved me. The feeling was mutual. He was my best friend. On many levels, I identified with Joe. Being extremely introverted, I was terribly awkward in social situations. I had an overactive blush mechanism wired into me and at the slightest provocation, turned bright red. It was impossible to control, and gave away my discomfort even when my behavior or lack of speech did not. So, I tended to be a loner. I never had many friends, and was not even very close to the few I had. If I had been a horse, I would have been standing by myself next to the pond, just like Joe.

Besides that, due to my insecurity, I was a little defensive and crotchety. I took slights and perceived insults very seriously. So I didn't particularly like people. They represented danger to me, and my sensitive psyche. It was better to lash out or avoid, rather than take any chances of getting hurt. Sometimes, that insecurity presented as arrogance. It's funny because I didn't *feel* better than anyone…I felt much worse. Why would false arrogance be my defense? I don't know. All I know is that animals were much easier to be around than people.

Animals never noticed or cared that I blushed, faltered over my words, was a klutz, or had ugly, frizzy hair. Animals didn't care that my older sister was brilliant and I was a sorry disappointment. Animals didn't care that I sucked my thumb till I was eight (or so) and that I could never tell my left from my right. Animals didn't care that I was shy. In fact, they seemed to like my quiet, gentle demeanor.

Yep, two peas in a pod, old Joe and me. If I could love Joe, the horse *nobody* loved, maybe even the least desirable of creatures *was* lovable. Maybe even me.

Joe and I needed each other. And Joe showed up at one of the most daunting times in anyone's life: middle school. People can be cruel, but few are crueler than during the middle school years. The cruelty towards others bothered me more than the cruelty towards me. I figured *I* deserved it.

I had a beautiful friend, Lynn. She was so gorgeous that she was a model, in fact. Because she was so lovely, all the middle school girls hated her. I was her only friend. I didn't fall in with the crowd since I was an outcast in my own right, so didn't follow their uniform jealousy of lovely Lynn.

To her great misfortune, she modeled not only clothes, but undergarments. The only thing more striking than the cruelty of a middle schooler is his immaturity. The middle school girls got a hold of a magazine picture of Lynn in a bra, showed it to the middle school boys, and soon it was circulating all over the school.

Now, had I been Lynn's folks, I might have anticipated this would be the result and decided that perhaps bra modeling would not be the best activity for a 6th grade girl. However, poor Lynn held her gorgeous head high and didn't show that this exposure bothered her. But I knew it did.

I was never the most wonderful of friends. I was not mean, but I didn't give my friends much of my time. Joe and Burton's Farm got the lion share of my time. Still, I was nice to Lynn, and she was grateful. Made me feel a little less like the weasel-face Mick was always badgering.

At any rate, middle school was not an easy time, particularly for anyone (like me) not in the center of the bell curve. I wish every struggling middle schooler had a horse like Joe. Joe saved me.

So, back to the story about my third serious injury at the farm, now that everyone is boo-hooing about how hard it was to be a misfit. It was a slow day at the farm, and I had finished my chores. After making sure with Milly that it would be ok for me to go off on a trail ride by myself, I raced out to the field.

Joe saw me coming, and nickered as he trotted up to me. As he reached me, he shoved his nose against my chest, and I wrapped my arms around him. This was a very typical greeting. He would exhale streams of warm air into my belly, while I leaned my head against his face, and scratched him behind his ears.

"Hello, my beautiful horse," I said.

Joe nibbled at my shirt.

I reached in my pocket and pulled out a carrot. He carefully swiped it off my palm, and munched happily. After I clambered aboard his back, he trotted to the barn. The mud was met with the usual hesitation, then the sucking, groaning passage. Burton had laid a series of planks across the mud, but it was almost more treacherous to try to get the horse to walk on the planks. They were invariably slippery, and teetered side to side with the horse's weight. If the horse slipped, which he did nearly always, he foundered even more spasmodically in the mud. There were some horses that went lame because of their struggles with the mud. It sure seems someone should have figured out a solution to the problem of the mud, but as far as I knew, no one ever did.

Anyway, we made it safely through the mud, and into the barn. I spent some time brushing Joe, trying to get as much of the mud off as I could. By this time, I'd learned how to clean his hooves with a hoof pick. I picked up each of his legs, and turned his hoof up so that I could pick out any stones or caked dirt stuck in them. I was bent over, concentrating on a hoof when Mick walked by.

He slammed (by accident) (*not*) into my bottom, and I smashed against Joe.

"Oops. Sorry," he said, with a nasty grin. Joe dropped his hoof onto my toe. It wasn't his fault. He quickly regained his balance, moving his weight in an instant off my poor toe. Then he nuzzled me, as if to apologize. My toe ached, but I didn't think it was broken. It had not been very nice of Mick, but I don't think he expected me to get hurt.

"Are you okay?" he asked quickly. He was glancing at Milly, who was at the far end of the barn. She looked up when I made a little groan of "ouch."

I didn't answer. For one thing, I was mad. For another, my toe kind of throbbed. For a third, if I accused him, he might get in trouble. And for a fourth, any show of concern from Mick, no matter how insincere, was welcome.

So, I nodded, and he scurried away. Milly almost looked like she was going to call him back, but then shook her head and returned to whatever work she was doing.

I finished picking Joe's hooves, then grabbed his hackamore out of the tack room. As I led him outside, Milly glanced up.

"Have a good ride," she called.

It was a windy day, and my hair was blowing all about, snapping across my eyes. Joe side-stepped a little as I mounted. I think the wind and blustery promise of a change in the weather had him a little unnerved. I crawled onto his back, and we headed out to the trail.

It was eerie on the trail. I don't know if it was the approaching storm, or my throbbing toe, or just something I ate. Whatever the source, I was a little spooked. Sometimes, when I was all alone in nature, I got that sensation. It was like someone was watching me. Even worse, I had the sense that someone was not only watching, but expected something of me.

I had no idea what the expectation entailed, but it was *palpable.* (I'd just learned that word and could hardly wait to use it, but you'd be surprised how hard it is to sneak it into regular conversation.)

Joe seemed to feel it too. The wind howled and whipped the tree branches near us. Joe began prancing and shaking his head. I wondered if that was God trying to talk to me. I didn't usually think much about God except every night right before going to sleep. At those times I prayed my all-inclusive prayer, "Bless everyone and everything. Amen, to angels and all." That was all that needed to be said, and I was proud of the economy of that catch-all prayer.

Sometimes, all alone in nature, I thought of God with fear and trembling. I figured if God were to materialize, and in my vivid imagination -- He was about to, it would be terrifying. The strangest part of these episodes was that I almost *wanted* Him to show Himself. I was simultaneously shaking in my boots and longing to see if He was real.

Well, this was one of those times. As we entered the forested section of the trail, I felt a *presence* watching me. My eyes darted about to the flapping branches, and I startled at every crack of the twigs hitting against each other.

Joe had been acting strangely from the beginning, but he likely picked up on my disquiet. He was always very attuned to my feelings, so it was not surprising that he became nervous too.

I peered into the forest around me, and even said out loud, "Who's there?" No one answered. I wanted to ask, *Is it you, God?* but was so afraid He would answer, that I didn't.

What if God did show up? Would He be pleased with me? I doubted it. I had not shown Him much care or attention in my first decade of life. We *had* gone to church when we lived in Memphis. If you lived in the Bible Belt during that time period and didn't go to church, everyone assumed you were a Commie, or worse, a heathen. However, the church we went to was the least objectionable to my atheist parents, and God was rarely mentioned. I never really listened to the sermons, anyway. The church worship center had huge plate glass windows that overlooked the Mississippi River, and was perfect for day-dreaming while the big, flat barges floated by.

So I shivered on Joe's back, thinking if God was real, and did materialize, I was going to have a heart attack. I was thinking of turning around and heading back to the barn without finishing the trail loop, when there was a loud crack.

My first thought was that God had smote me. I did remember the word "smote" from my church-going days. I wasn't sure what all was entailed in being smote, but I knew *none* of it was good. Joe might have thought God was smiting us as well, because he leaped into the air, and then barreled into the forest. I don't know why he chose to run away into the forest. Horses are creatures of habit, and it would have made much more sense to stay on the trail. For whatever reason, he didn't. Branches reached out with stinging witch hands and clutched at me. The wind roared with demonic laughter, the branches snaked out, and the wild, crazed Joe weaved through the underbrush.

Well, I was a better rider than I had been a year ago, but I could not withstand the sudden swerves in conjunction with the trees grabbing me. Joe pivoted suddenly. I slammed into a thick branch and was smacked to the ground.

I landed on my hand, and unfortunately, my finger didn't remain properly aligned as I crashed down. It bent back, there was a flash of excruciating pain, and all the wind was knocked out of me. When I sat up, I almost passed out with the pain in my middle finger. I am a pain-wimp. Pain and I do not get along.

I swayed, a little woozy as I looked at my finger. It may well have been mild shock. The finger was already swollen to three times its normal size with a whole rainbow of colors one doesn't ever want to see in human skin.

Worse yet, I was at least a mile or so from the barn, and my loyal, devoted horse was gone. I was more distraught over *that* than my obviously broken finger. Standing up slowly, other achy parts yelped at me. Careful assessment of all my parts: a little scratched up, and bruised, but otherwise unbroken. Walking slowly back to the barn, I realized my aching toe might have been hurt more than just a little bit when Joe clomped on it. I felt mighty sorry for myself. The good news: all my fear that God might appear had vanished. Now, I just thought about how surely I was going to die of pain before I made it back to the barn.

I trudged along, wiping muddy tears from my cheeks, and praying Joe was okay. What direction had he run? Had I blacked out momentarily upon falling? He had vanished before I sat up and looked around.

The storm was definitely getting closer. The clouds were ominous. If there was anything more fearful than God materializing when I was all alone in nature, it was a tornado doing so. Unfortunately, in tornado alley, where Chicago had its unlucky home, the tornado was more likely to appear than God.

So I walked as quickly as I could, but honestly, everything hurt, I was scared, and the wind was against me. Singing often keeps up my spirits, but the only song that came to mind was, *Nobody loves me, everybody hates me, guess I'll just eat worms.*

I don't know how long I was traipsing along in that miserable condition, when the pounding of approaching horses' hooves broke through my self-pity. Was Joe returning? I looked up, swatting the streaming tears away. It was Mick, astride a trail horse, leading Joe.

"Are you okay?" he asked, for the second time that day. (This would get a few asterisks and underlinings in my journal that night.)

This time, he looked like he meant it. He actually appeared to be worried.

"I don't think so," I said, and the tears started afresh.

"When Joe came back alone, we thought something must have happened."

I waited. I expected him to add the usual rejoinder: something along the lines of "and we figured he got a look at your face and made a dash for it." But he didn't. He didn't add a single nasty epithet.

"Is anything broken?"

(Besides your mind?) Nope, he didn't add that, either.

"I think I broke my finger." I held it up. Now I was not flipping him the bird, but it did look like that to a casual observer. My middle finger of my right hand had ballooned to a scary size, and I held it up to show him.

Now the Mick I knew regained control of his mouth, "Well same to you, hay-head."

He chuckled, and hopped off his horse.

"I think you're right. If it's not broken, it's got a small whale growing inside of it. I'll help you up on Joe."

He held Joe's reins while cupping his hands to give me a knee up. I was dubious. If Mick were offering me a knee up, I did not think it unlikely that he would throw me clear over Joe so he could laugh as I landed in a broken heap on the other side.

I paused.

"C'mon," he said, "What are you waiting for? An engraved invitation?"

"My hand really hurts," I said, "I don't know if I can hold the reins."

Mick looked at me with pity, as though he wondered how many times the human race could produce someone with my deficits and still survive.

"You have *two* hands, or did you forget about the other one?"

I actually *had* forgotten about the other one. I always neck-reined with my right hand, but currently could not move my right hand without terrible pain.

"Oh."

Mick muttered something under his breath, and shook his cupped hands at me.

"Sometime this year?"

I bent my knee and he heaved me onto Joe's back.

Shaking his head, he mounted his own horse and we headed slowly back to the barn.

I wasn't about to speak sternly to Joe in Mick's presence, but I confess I was a little miffed. Why had the horse who loved me run away, without even a glance back? Admittedly, fear can do gruesome things to folks. I wet my pants in third grade rather than dare ask the teacher if I could go to the bathroom. Believe me, I understood fear. Still.

Joe flicked his ears back as though he could hear my inner voice. Then he did the most amazing thing. He stopped, twisted his head around and looked at me. He was waiting for something from me. We gazed at each other, and an understanding sparked across the gap.

"I forgive you," I said.

"For what, hay-head? Helping a dork?" Mick called back.

Chapter Fourteen

The broken finger hardly affected my farm work. It was splinted and six weeks later, the splint came off, and I was good as new. The knuckle was about double the size it had been, but other than that, there were no other traces of the fall. Joe was exceedingly careful with me after that, and he never shied (so drastically) again. I think he knew he had done some damage, and felt bad about it.

Milly suggested that we kids join 4-H. She would supply the animals we would need. She felt it would be a great experience. There were all kinds of 4-H classes and shows. There were even horse shows and Milly told us she'd be willing to cart horses to shows for us in her horse trailer. Both Debby and I joined 4-H. Debby wanted to show Rockabye. I decided I would do a 4-H dog training class, and then show Lady, my sweet Dalmatian. Peeper joined us as well. Mick found it all beneath him and wasn't interested in being a part of it. Milly told me there were driving competitions and she felt Joe would do very well in that.

"There's also Western Pleasure classes, but you couldn't do that with Joe since he won't take a saddle. But you could choose one of the other horses." So we joined 4-H with great expectations.

She may have had an ulterior motive. It was around this time that she inherited a big black and white bunny. One of her children brought it home from school. She in turn brought it to the farm specifically with the intent of pawning it off on a gullible farm kid. As I have intimated already, I was the Queen of Gullible.

I was enamored with the bunny. All animals captivated me. As I reached in the hutch, petting the bunny, she told me that 4-H had lots of classes including rabbit conformation. Was she kidding? She wasn't. People raise bunnies just like any show animal to be the perfect representation of its breed. This bunny, Thumper, was a Checkered Giant. Milly said he was the most beautiful Checkered Giant she had ever seen.

I agreed, though he was the *only* Checkered Giant I had ever seen. She continued telling me about all his finer points, then added, "I bet he'd win a 4-H class in his breed conformation."

I continued petting him. His fur was so soft, and his sweet little pink nose continual twitching so endearing. Milly now swooped in for the kill.

"If you want him, you can have him. And I'll even give you the hutch for free."

Well, unlike the offer of Rockabye the year before, my parents could not possibly refuse this. There would be no boarding cost, and rabbits don't eat much. (Do they?)

There was only one objection I could anticipate my parents raising.

"What about the winter? I don't think my parents would let me keep him in the house."

"Oh, look at his thick fur. He'll be fine in the hutch over the winter."

I was not at all sure that was true. However, with all my facts now lined up, I went home and told my parents the good news.

They also voiced some concern about the winter, as they didn't want the rabbit in the house. When I assured them the rabbit would live very happily in the hutch outdoors, they approved the plan. They were very supportive of the idea of 4-H, and glad to have me learn how to train Lady in the 4-H dog classes.

We drove the van to the farm, loaded up the hutch and Thumper, and just like that, I was the proud owner of a prize Checkered Giant.

Thumper had all kinds of fascinating habits and endearing qualities. First of all, he was almost care-free. I fed him some special rabbit food each day, and his poop dropped out of a screened bottom. There was really very little work involved.

I could even let him loose in the house at times. We locked Lady outside, and then let Thumper hop around the living room. He did occasionally poop, but he was a very clean rabbit. He would clean that up himself by eating it. I don't know if all rabbits are so conscientious but like Milly said, he was a prize winning Checkered Giant.

I read about what was involved in the rabbit breed class. All I had to do was wear a white lab coat, and carry him to the judging table. For the show, he had to be handled in a specified manner, which was explicitly described. That special handling demonstrated that I had control over the rabbit. He had to be clean, with trimmed nails. Other than that, he just had to look beautiful while he was judged. This sounded within my capabilities so when the Competition Registration came out, I signed up for the Checkered Giant Breed, and the Dog Obedience Events. I decided to hold off on the horse events till the next competition. Showing two animals at one contest was all I should tackle at first.

Meanwhile, I started the 4-H dog training classes. Lady was a willing student, and the things I learned probably would prevent similar disasters as the *baby Holly on the sled* incident. With Debby and I jointly involved in 4-H, we reached a truce of sorts. At least I didn't hate her as much, but that could be because I was more mature now at the ripe old age of eleven going on twelve. Maybe the love of Joe and my growing competence with a whole variety of farm duties and animals was slowly transforming me. I no longer needed to hate her to give me a reason to get up in the morning. She was no longer the threat to my self-esteem as she had been when I was nine. Her teeth still outpaced the rest of her face.

The first 4-H show finally arrived. I eagerly brought Thumper in a little traveling cage to the fairgrounds. He had to spend his time at the fair in a numbered cage, alongside all the other Checkered Giants. If I had not known his number, I would not have known which one he was. All the Checkered Giants looked exactly the same. (I bet they think the same thing about us humans.)

Thumper had to hang out in the cage for quite some time while people walked by and gawked at him. He didn't seem to mind. He put his best rabbit foot forward for the judging. When it was time for me to bring him to meet the judge, I donned my white coat. I picked him up in the prescribed rabbit handling manner and carried him to the table. As I set him down in front of the judges, he began to go crazy. He scratched at me, not out of meanness, but it was all unfamiliar to him. Somehow, I managed to calm him, but not before he had drawn a little blood on my wrist with his neatly trimmed nails. The judges exchanged some quick glances with each other, and I wondered if they saw the blood dripping on their show table. Thumper performed flawlessly for the entire rest of the time. He strutted his stuff like the perfectly conformed Checkered Giant that he was.

Then I returned him to his cage, and watched the other 4-H contestants bring their rabbits to the judging table. It was a nail biting moment when the judges came to award the winners their ribbons.

Thumper won a blue ribbon. Now, this was surprising, since there had been that moment when he had scuffled with me. I guess the judges were giving me credit for bringing the dangerous rabbit back under control. Before you are too impressed, in 4-H, lots of kids get blue ribbons in each class. The participants are not in competition with each other. They are in competition with themselves against a pre-designated standard. As long as they meet the standard, they get the reward.

Even at the tender age of eleven, life was often a rat-race, with one person winning (rarely me), and someone else losing (often me.) How refreshing to know that as long as I did what was expected of me, I would receive the prize. I was overjoyed to have won a ribbon, especially since I didn't have to do anything but hold my rabbit.

Lady won a blue ribbon too. She really did do a good job in her obedience class. She had to sit, heel, and stay. The hardest part was the extended stay when I backed away a full long leash length and told her, *Down*. She had almost never stayed down during her training classes. She was a friendly dog, and saw no reason not to come and lick her mistress most of the time. So when the extended stay command was given, her obedience was tested to the utmost. I chewed my lower lip.

She lay down along with about twenty other dogs in the class. Then all of us stepped back after saying, "Stay." If the dog got up, and didn't stay, you lost any hope of a blue ribbon, even in that encouraging environment. Lady stayed however, and secured her blue ribbon. Victoriously, my rabbit and my dog came home from our first 4-H contest.

I didn't have much to do with Thumper after that. I had so many constraints on my time with the farm. I took him out on a leash occasionally to let him munch clover, and he did indeed live outside through two brutal winters. Someone offered me money for him, but talked a lot about how "big and juicy" he looked so I told him, "No thanks." That was Thumper's one and only show. Why sully his blue ribbon streak?

I wanted to try the horse classes at the next 4-H show. They occurred regularly, and there was one near the end of the following spring.

Milly told me that would be fine. She asked which horse I might like to use for the Western Pleasure Class.

"Joe," I told her.

"You can't use Joe," she reminded me, "For Western Pleasure, the horse has to be saddled."

"I know," I said.

"Vicky, Joe hasn't allowed anyone near him with a saddle in ten years. He almost killed the last person that tried to get one on him."

I looked at Milly and didn't say anything.

"Why would you want to even try? You and Joe are doing so well, and he's come such a long way."

I still didn't answer. I am not sure I *knew* why. One thing was certain: I didn't want to ride any other horse in my 4-H classes. Joe was the best horse in the world, and the horse I trusted more than any other.

"If I can't ride Joe in Western Pleasure, I don't think I want to do the class," I said.

She looked at me, with a mixture of bemusement and incredulity.

"Well, it's up to you. I guess if anyone could talk Joe into taking a saddle, it would be you. But I don't want you to try it when I am not around, deal?"

"Deal," I agreed.

Vicky Kaseorg

Chapter Fifteen

The idea of how to best help Joe accept a saddle percolated in my brain for a while. Winter set in, and I had several months to consider the problem before spring horse shows commenced. I perused the list of 4-H classes at the show I wanted to attend. Both Western Pleasure, and Pleasure Pony Driving sounded interesting. Barrel Racing was an option as well. Did I dare give that a shot? Who could teach me to barrel race? Well, the obvious answer didn't seem likely. Would Mick agree to show me what to do, the inept hay-hair that he hated? It wouldn't hurt to ask. I mentioned my hopes to Milly, who nodded but didn't offer an opinion. It was not a closely guarded secret that she felt Joe was unlikely to take a saddle.

Since it was winter, we had lots of spare time. It was often too cold to ride, or too treacherous with all the snow and ice. So the kids would sit in the one heated place in the barn, the tack and soda machine room. We snuggled there under horse blankets in between chores to warm up. My

134

favorite chore on the bitter cold days was milking Cindy or Matilda. Their teats were warm, and my fingertips were always cold.

I always brought Joe in the barn when I could. There was no free standing stall that winter, and it broke my heart to see him out in the cold. He really never seemed to mind, though. He had a very thick, scraggly winter coat. Anyway, I had come in to the tack room to warm up after brushing Joe.

Debby and Mick sat on one hay bale together. Milly was in there, too. I sat on another hay bale, soaking in the warmth.

"Mick, Vicky needs your help," Milly said.

I do? What was she up to now?

Mick looked at her with his mouth hanging open. He seemed as surprised by her statement as me, and a whole lot less happy about it. Incredible Incisors Debby smirked, and ever so imperceptibly elbowed him.

"She wants to enter Joe in the barrel racing class for the summer 4-H show. I thought you could help teach her."

"She needs a saddle," Mick said instantly, with an undisguised burst of relief washing over his face, "So she couldn't enter Joe in that one."

"She feels that won't be a problem," Milly said.

"She also feels that Joe is not an ugly old nag."

"Mick..." Milly admonished, wagging her finger at him.

"If she doesn't die getting a saddle on him, I'll show her how to barrel race," he promised. He grinned with a knowing glance at Debby, and I suspected he didn't think he was in any danger of having to teach me anything.

"How does that sound, Vicky?" Milly asked.

"I'll try not to die," I said solemnly.

I needed to get right to work if I had any hope of convincing Joe to let me get a saddle on him. I had almost never been in a saddle myself. Having learned to ride bareback, it was frankly my preference. Yet, if I was to try a class as fast and challenging as barrel racing, I would need to practice in a saddle. This was not going to be a cakewalk to a blue ribbon like my bunny conformation class had been.

I had certainly watched enough barrel races, and knew what was generally involved. Specifics on the class were fuzzy, but now Mick was being forced to teach me those. So, I stood up. "May as well start now."

Milly laughed.

"No one can accuse you of grass growing under your feet."

That expression has been applied to me thousands of times. Milly was right. If I knew something needed to be done, I hated waiting. It must be done immediately. This personality trait has some definite benefits, but also some very challenging drawbacks. No one can ever do things soon enough or early enough in my book. You can imagine how wearying this is to less driven people, like...the rest of the world.

"What saddle should I use?" I asked.

Mick was just staring at me like I had three heads.

"Does your mother ever wish she could send you back?' he asked.

"Mick!" Milly shrieked, as she handed me a saddle.

"I don't mean that in a nasty way," he said.

This seemed to pacify Milly, though I was struggling to understand what non-nasty way he could have meant it.

Milly followed me out of the tack room. Joe was in his usual place in the central barn room, tied to the ring on the wall.

"It's ok, Milly," I told her, "I'm not going to go very near today. You don't have to worry."

I really didn't want her watching. I have never been very good with an audience. Joe and I could *certainly* work through this saddle business if it was just me and him. Uncertainty most often reared its traumatizing head when I was on display.

She understood, and returned to the tack room. Debby and Mick giggled, standing at the door watching. Milly shooed them back in the tack room, and closed the door.

Joe knew something was up. He perked his ears forward as he saw me with the saddle in my arms. Then he flicked them back. He stomped his front hoof. No, even me, his beloved friend, was an enemy with a saddle in my arms. He flicked his tail back and forth.

I stopped on the other side of the barn, and put the saddle down with a thump. Then I sat on it. Joe looked puzzled, and his ears pointed forward again. Even he was wondering what I was up to. Without looking at him, I just sat on the saddle, quietly contemplating the icicles hanging from the front beam above the barn door.

Milly popped out about twenty minutes later. I was still sitting on the saddle...freezing, by the way, but I didn't let on. Joe had become bored and was munching on some stray wisps of hay.

"Looks like a good strategy," she said.

I nodded.

"Ready to help feed?"

I nodded again, and stood up.

"May I leave the saddle here while I help with the hay?" I asked.

She smiled. "I like the way you think, Vicky."

I don't know what I would have done without Milly as my ally. She whistled through her teeth, and Mick and Peeper, trailed by Debby emerged. Mick scaled the ladder into the hay loft and tossed down some bales while the rest of us ripped them open and began dispersing them to the horses in the barn. I brought Joe his dinner first. He glanced at the saddle, but his ears remained forward. Every few bites of hay, he raised his head and looked at the saddle. Since the saddle made no move to come closer, he returned to his dinner.

Mick passed me with arms filled with hay. "Good for you. At this rate, you should have the saddle within a foot of him by next winter."

I ignored him. He was possibly correct. This was not the way I liked to do things. It would require patience, and I am not normally patient, as you have already seen. However, enough had been forced on Joe in his sorry past to last a lifetime. I was not going to force the saddle on him, but would wait until he asked for it. Who knew how long that might be? Still, it was the only way I wouldn't destroy his trust in me.

When we finished feeding the barn horses, Burton had pulled the tractor and flat-bed up for us to load for the outdoor feeding. I untied Joe, and was about to walk him out to let him into the pasture. He paused and turned his head to look at the saddle. Then he stepped toward it. I let out his lead. He moved a few cautious steps nearer the saddle, blowing air out his flaring nostrils. A foot away from it, he lowered his head and sniffed. I was silent. Joe was making peace of some sort, and I didn't want to jinx it.

Mick was returning from loading hay on the flatbed, so I gently pulled on Joe's lead and clicked my tongue.

"Come on, pretty horse, time to go."

He followed me quietly.

In the winter the mud patch was frozen, and the horses had an easier time crossing it. He nuzzled me goodbye, and picked his way across the frozen patch. Then with a flick of his tail, he cantered away. His tail streamed behind him. He suddenly kicked up his heels, bucking. How funny! Like a colt, dancing in the cold.

I returned to the barn and hoisted a hay bale, then headed to the flat-bed. The other workers were all helping load the hay, but they drifted away when that task was done. It was just me and Mick jostling alone on the hay run to the pasture.

As usual, Mick didn't speak to me. The cold was seeping into me now, after all that time sitting. I glanced across the field and saw Joe was now walking. His capering had ended. He was headed to the far pasture, having already had his dinner. The other horses came nickering and trotting to the feed bin, nipping and shoving each other for the prime position.

As we tossed the hay into the bin, I watched Joe, all by himself in the distance. He had stopped and raised his head, sniffing the frosty air. Even from this distance, I could see the white puffs from his nostrils. The sun was setting, and an orange, magenta glow settled over the landscape. Joe stood, with that heavenly backdrop, his mane flowing down his neck, his dark hair reflecting the sun's brilliant colors.

How could anyone call him ugly? My heart burst with love for this horse, all alone on the hillside with the sun blazing its glory across his swayed back.

Chapter Sixteen

Over the next month, I repeated my strategy with the saddle. Each time I plopped the saddle on the ground, I moved it just a few inches closer. Mick complained, because sometimes it was in his way. He growled and kicked at it, when he walked by.

"When God made you, he broke the mold," he snarled.

I thought perhaps he was complimenting me, as I sat there so patiently on the saddle on the floor.

"And that was a huge relief to mankind," Mick added.

So maybe it wasn't a compliment.

I didn't lose heart. Joe almost never flicked his ears back now when he saw me with the saddle. It became a part of the room for him, and seemed to pose no threat, so he largely ignored it.

After sitting on the saddle a while, I inched it a little closer and then brushed Joe. He loved to be brushed, particularly as the winter slowly began to be a little less icy, and the spring thaw was just around the corner. His winter coat was shedding - probably a little itchy. He rubbed his head furiously against my front, and practically purred with delight when I scratched him behind his ears.

The deadline for the 4-H entry form submission was approaching. I had still not gotten the saddle within four feet of Joe. Should I commit the entry fee on such an uncertain venture? It was not a huge amount of money, but it was non-refundable.

Finally deciding it was worth taking the chance, I submitted my entry and my money. I entered the three classes I'd been interested in, knowing Joe was only ready for the driving class. Well, *he* was ready for the Barrel Racing, but I sure wasn't.

It was time for the next stage of his saddle training. I grabbed a saddle pad out of the tack room, and walked straight over to Joe. He tossed his head when I stopped in front of him, sniffing the blanket. I watched his ears. Still forward. Slowly, I moved next to his side. He turned his head nibbling at the blanket, but remained unperturbed. I began rubbing his side with the blanket, watching him carefully. Even I was a little surprised at how nonchalantly he was handling the touch of the saddle pad against him.

Slowly, I lifted the far edge and carefully, with my hand rubbing across his back under the pad, laid it over him. He didn't flinch at all. Smoothing the blanket with my hands, I gently pressed down all over his back. He did not react at all.

Leaving the blanket on his back, I reached into my pocket and gave him a few more extra carrots than usual. While doing my chores, the blanket remained there on his back. He didn't seem to notice or care at all. This was very good!

The next day, I repeated the steps with the pad, and then unhooked his lead from the wall and walked him around the barn. We walked up to the saddle, which was now only three feet in front of him. I took a carrot out of my pocket and put it on the saddle. Now this did concern him. He wanted the carrot, but he snorted a bit. He couldn't quite make sense of the carrot on the saddle.

Mick, *of course*, chose that moment to walk into the barn. He saw the carrot on the saddle, and Joe snorting with some consternation.

"I hope you write a book about your training techniques," Mick said, "I bet all the other psychos would buy it."

Joe seemed to come to a decision, and tentatively reached his head down toward the saddle. He stretched his muzzle as far it would go, and knocked the carrot off the saddle. Then he gobbled it off the floor.

Laughing, I placed another carrot on the saddle. This time, he stretched his muzzle, and slowly closed his mouth around the carrot while it was still on the saddle. His mouth left a wet smudge on the saddle. The third time I offered a carrot on the saddle, he snatched it without hesitation. In doing so, he'd stepped a foot closer. The saddle was within two feet of him. Progress!

I stood with him in that position, for some time, stroking his neck and scratching his ears. Peeper catapulted by and glanced over.

"Why are you just standing there?" she asked, slamming on her brakes.

I kept stroking Joe's neck, and shrugged my shoulders. I didn't want to speak during this magical moment.

"Cause she's mental," Mick said, leading a horse through the barn. The horse's back hoof nicked the saddle and it rocked for a second. Joe's head flew up, but he immediately calmed, and closed his eyes again.

Now I don't want you to get the idea that Mick only picked on *me*. He had a mischievous (okay, evil) bent with *any* potential victim. Still, as long as I wasn't the sole object of his warped humor, I actually found him amusing.

It was the older kids' responsibility to answer the phone and take the reservations for trail rides. Mick did not love leading trails, and there were times he sabotaged his own parents' business. When they were out of earshot, and he answered the phone, he often barked, "Pete's Funeral Home. You plug 'em, we plant 'em." I know it is infantile but even fifty years later, remembering that, I chuckle.

He used to shake the soda cans, and then clap his arm around unsuspecting young workers.

"I bought this for you," he'd say.

"Thanks," said the unsuspecting victim (who, by the way, more than once was me.)

As soon as the victim opened the can, it spurted like Old Faithful, all over the victim's face. Mick collapsed in peals of laughter. Sometimes Burton caught him in these pranks, and he belted Mick. Not often, however. Mick had a well-honed sense of timing, and managed to pull off impossible feats of subversive pranks without ever being caught. I thought

Mick had a high probability of embarking on a successful life of crime. He was that good.

While I was standing with Joe in front of the saddle, the phone rang. Mick had finished shoving the horse he'd been leading into a stall, and ran to grab the phone.

"Hello? Hello? I don't know why you are calling at a time like this, but it isn't funny." Then he hung up, bowled over with laughter. Apparently, it *was* funny.

The phone rang again.

"Hallo," he said in a Dutch sounding accent, "Vee are here to help you, yah."

I giggled despite my best efforts not to. It was all stupid, I agree, but there was something about Mick's continual irreverence that tickled me.

The phone rang a third time. Mick snatched it off the hook.

"Burton's Farm," he said seriously. He listened with a wicked grin on his face, nodding, "Oh we get that all the time. I think you must have dialed the wrong number. Yeh, I'd be annoyed too. Totally childish."

It's a wonder Burton's Farm survived Mick. I should have told on him, but I never did. He deserved it for sure, with how horribly he treated me, but somehow, I couldn't bring myself to turn him in. For one thing, I knew his punishment if Burton got wind of his pranks would be harsh. But for another, even as the brunt of his jokes, Mick made me laugh.

I led Joe out of the barn, with the saddle pad on his back. We headed over to the riding ring. I needed the mounting block for my next plan. Steering Joe next to the block, I carefully lowered myself on the pad. Joe was completely nonchalant. The pad weighed next to nothing, didn't creak like a saddle would, and with his deep sway back, didn't even shift much. I knew it might slide off if he went fast, so we just looped the ring once at a walk, and then I slid off with the blanket at the gate.

We returned to the barn. I laid the pad on top of the saddle. Joe sniffed it. He seemed to be deep in thought as he looked at the pad, atop the saddle.

"Ok, buddy, now let's try something new." I picked up the pad and carefully put it back on his back. He flicked his ears, looking at the saddle. Then I removed the pad and returned it to the top of the saddle. After I'd done this several times, he didn't flinch at all when the pad plopped on his back.

I tied him to the ring on the wall, with the pad on his back and the saddle now right in front of him. Moment of truth. I went to the saddle, slowly kneeled down, and picked it up.

Joe didn't startle or move. He sniffed the saddle like he had a thousand times by now. Slowly I moved to his side, saddle in hand. He flicked his tail, and turned his head to glance at me.

Slowly, very slowly, I hefted the saddle higher, and as gently as I could, settled it on his back. I was holding my breath. Joe's ears swiveled, and I almost expected him to explode bucking as he had so long ago with Mick. But he didn't. He stood still.

A deep sigh whooshed out of me as I reached into my pocket for carrots. He munched happily while I stroked his nose. The saddle sat like a trophy on his deeply swayed back. I hadn't cinched it yet. I considered doing so, but then decided this was enough for today. Mick and Peeper had disappeared. No one had seen this moment of triumph. It was my secret for now. My and *Joe's* secret. Joe nuzzled me, asking for another carrot.

Chapter Seventeen

One terrible cold or flu felled me each year. I never missed a day at the farm no matter how harsh the weather, unless I had a fever. I probably would have dragged myself there, but my mom, even with her Benign Neglect, would not let me go to the farm with a fever.

The only benefit of being sick was I had time to read. I loved to read and was a voracious reader. I was determined to read every book in the library. To that end, I decided I would read a book by every author, in alphabetical order. Quickly determining that I would not make it past the A's with that strategy, my plan required slight adjustment: read one author from each letter of the alphabet. Once I made it through the alphabet, I'd start over and it would have to be a different author with each letter.

This would have been a great plan except I got quickly bogged down in the F's. If you are a horse lover then you know why. Walter Farley was the author of the Black Stallion series, the best horse books ever written. I fell in love with the black stallion and could not get enough of reading about him. Fortunately, Farley wrote several books in the series. I was heart-broken when I reached the end of the series, and had to move on to G. However, I didn't start reading my G author until I had finished every Black Stallion book.

Fortunately H came right after G and I got to read Marguerite Henry and the wonderful Misty of Chincoteague series. I hatched a plan that one day I would visit Chincoteague and find the wild ponies described in that book myself. (A half century later, I finally fulfilled that dream.)

Wonderful as those horse books were, the cold that toppled me as the winter was sputtering to an end was terrible to endure. I was a millimeter from my goal of riding Joe with a saddle, and was now waylaid by the common cold. *Oh bitter, bitter life!*

Fortunately, when I was better, the weather had taken a favorable turn. Spring was in the air! That meant the farm's busy time was revving up. Trail rides would be recommencing soon. As an experienced trail guide now at the ripe old age of twelve, I would be busy as well. I needed to get that saddle on Joe!

I hurried back to the farm with sniffles subsiding. Joe was overjoyed to see me, or at least to see my apple slices and carrots. He was shedding his shaggy coat in great tufts of hair. The frozen mud pit melted and became the gaping jaws of danger again. Baby goats were being born, and little chicks suddenly appeared along with the daffodils.

We resumed the saddle training where I had left off. Joe didn't seem to have lost any ground. I flung the pad off and on his back, making it land with a little more vigor each time. When he didn't shy at all from the blanket thwacking him, I laid the saddle gently on the pad. He seemed nonplussed. Ok. Girth time.

Milly was concerned that he might kick me as I reached under him to grab the girth so she stood on one side, and she carefully handed it under his belly to me. Joe was remarkably calm. In fact, his eyes were closed. I slowly tightened the girth, inch by inch. His eyes opened, but he didn't otherwise move.

I tightened it enough that the saddle wouldn't slip, but not as tight as it would need to be for me to ride him. Milly stepped back and nodded.

"I think he is going to be okay," she said.

Taking the lead from her, I walked Joe out of the barn, with the loosely cinched saddle on his back. I wish I had a picture of that moment. Unfortunately, the paparazzi were busy elsewhere. Mick and Debby looked up from chatting at their perch on a hay bale and fell silent. Milly followed me, and Debby and Mick followed her. I really didn't want an audience, but I didn't blame them for wanting to see this. Everyone was pretty sure there would be equine fireworks and no one wanted to miss it.

When I reached the riding ring, Debby and Mick climbed onto the top fence rail. Milly stood by the gate. She opened it for me, without a word.

I led Joe in. He plodded along as though this was not the most pivotal day of his life. The sky was blue, with puffy clouds skittering across it. It was not exactly warm yet, but the air had no bite in it anymore. A chicken with her brood of fluffy chicks were pecking at the ground just outside the riding ring, near the corner of the barn. Old, weathered wood with one rotted edge of the board left a hole in the lower wall, where the brood suddenly disappeared. The smell of life just about to burst forth wafted on the breeze.

I stopped and petted Joe's neck. He looked at me with his gentle brown eyes. There was not an ounce of panic or fear. Just kindness. I petted his side, rubbing away tufts of winter hair. *Carefully now, slowly tighten the cinch.* Joe's ears flicked back for a second and I cooed to him, "Good boy, Joe."

Then I lowered the stirrup inch by inch so that I could reach it. Grasping a hold of the saddle horn, I put my foot in the stirrup and holding my breath, hoisted myself up. As gently as I could I lowered myself in the saddle. Joe stood quietly, the skin on his shoulders twitching as a fly landed. I stroked his neck, and gathered my reins.

Softly, I touched my heels to his sides.

"Walk, Joe."

Joe walked forward, peacefully, as though this were just another typical day and not a small miracle.

"Trot, Joe."

He broke into a trot. I am sorry to say that being on a saddle didn't make his incredibly jarring trot any easier to sit than being bareback. For all I loved about Joe, I never loved his trot. It was one of the bounciest trots I have ever ridden.

If anything was going to make Joe buck me off, it would be my weight slamming down on his back with that impossible trot. However, he never made any move to buck, nor any complaint about the still terrible rider on his back.

"Canter, Joe."

Gratefully, he slipped into his effortless canter. If you are not a horse rider, there is probably no way to convey the joy of riding a cantering horse. The wind streaks though your hair, and it falls rhythmically on the back of your neck like the beat of a song. The horse's hooves clatter like a waltz, and you rock on the saddle in cadence with the rise and fall of the horse's neck. There is none of the jarring of the trot. The world whizzes by, but not with the frenzy of a gallop. It is pure, exhilarating joy to canter.

I looped the ring twice at a canter. I could have cantered forever. When I pulled up to the gate, Mick and Debby were gone. If there was nothing to gloat about, I guess they saw no reason to stay. Milly beamed at me.

"If I hadn't seen it, I wouldn't have believed it," she said.

I smiled back at her, about as happy as I'd ever been in my life.

"If you are going to win the Western Pleasure class, you are going to need to learn to sit his trot."

"I know."

"Think of softening your lower back. Let your bottom rock on the saddle more."

I nodded. Urging Joe forward again, I pressed my heels into him. He trotted. I tried to do as Milly suggested. For brief moments I had the feel of it, but it would take an act of God for me to be able to sit Joe's trot.

"Better!" she called.

The next time I circled the ring, she was gone too. Back to the never-ending work of the farm. I felt a little guilty for taking the time to ride while there was so much work to be done, but no way was I going to get off my horse too soon. This long awaited moment had to be savored. I rode Joe in the ring for about an hour, practicing all his gaits, stopping, changing leads, and all the things I would be asked to do in the Western Pleasure class.

Joe was flawless, though not nearly as easy to ride as Rockabye, nor as immediately responsive. Nonetheless, riding Joe in a saddle was the most satisfying experience of my life. There are not many things that I've been told cannot be done that I have then been able to do. It was almost anti-climactic, the aplomb with which he eased back into a saddle.

I never did learn to sit Joe's trot. I would never be a *great* rider on the back of Joe. *Grateful. Yes.* I would always be a *grateful* rider, and I think maybe that was better.

Chapter Eighteen

"Now, first you have to know that barrel racing is dangerous and you could die. Are you good with that?" Mick grinned at me as he rolled the barrels into place. We were going to walk the course first.

I nodded. In case you have missed the gist of my interactions with Mick, they consisted of him mocking me and me nodding. Still smitten, I was completely tongue-tied around him.

In barrel racing, an athletic horse and rider go as fast as they can in a clover-leaf pattern around three barrels. Mick was an amazing barrel racer. He was fearless, which is a necessary component of a good barrel racer. The best horses skim the edge of the barrel, leaning over at precarious angles that no one seems likely to survive.

Interestingly, barrel racing developed as a woman's sport. Men were off doing manly things like roping little baby cows and throwing them to the ground.

The barrel race begins with the rider shrieking at his horse at the top of his lungs because he must be going top speed as he reaches the start line. From there, excitement accelerates.

The horse can choose either the left or right barrel first. He must swing around the barrel at top speed, hugging the barrel as closely as possible. Horses that swung too wide around the barrel lose precious milliseconds. The best horses were not only agile and fast, but intelligent. That's why Joe was such a good barrel racer. He had all three of those qualities.

While it may seem that the rider contributes nothing to barrel racing but to hang on, that isn't true. The position and strength of the rider's legs actually contribute to the stability of the horse in those dizzying turns around the barrel. That's why Mick was such a good barrel racer. He was a very intuitive rider. His sense of how to adjust his body to compensate for the horse's movements was uncanny. Mick was a truly gifted rider, with balance that was innate. No one *learns* to ride like Mick. I was convinced he was born with it.

I think part of why Mick despised me so much was I didn't have that innate talent. I was not a natural horse rider. Never graceful, or fluid, or poetry in motion. As my older sister so frequently reminded me, I was a klutz.

But I had something Mick didn't have: compassion for the horse. So Joe loved me, and let me do things on him that he refused to let Mick do. I think that goaded Mick to no end.

If the horse ran past a barrel, without completing the pattern, it was a "no time" run and he was disqualified. He had to complete the pattern as fast as possible. If the racer hit the barrel and knocked it over, there was a penalty of five seconds. For top-notch barrel racers, this would be devastating. Thus, the best racers skimmed the barrels, but did not dislodge them. The best horses knew exactly how close to cut it.

In Burton's Farm shows, barrel racers could be bareback, which is how Mick could race Joe. But in the 4-H shows, and any sanctioned horse show, the rider had to be on saddle.

Mick walked the course with me. "Now pea-brain, Joe prefers to take the right barrel first. If you just let Joe have his head, he will do well despite you, Vicky."

The pea-brain line would have stung a bit since I am sensitive about my extremely small head. However, instead of focusing on the insult, I was wonderstruck that he had used my actual name. I think that was a first.

Joe watched us, as we walked the course. He was tied to the fence, all saddled and ready.

"You get the idea?" Mick asked.

I nodded.

We walked back to Joe, and I untied him. I stuck my foot in the stirrup, and with my usual lack of grace, managed to mount. Mick rolled his eyes, but refrained from his usual insults.

Mick used his toe to draw a line in the sand.

"This will be the starting line," he said, "You will come roaring through the gate at top speed by the time you hit the starting line."

"That sounds dangerous," I said.

He looked at me with barely concealed disdain, "Well you could stay home and knit baby booties instead."

"I just mean, what if people are standing in the way?"

"Then you plow through them."

I laughed. It never failed. He was so incorrigible but he always made me laugh.

"Now, once you kill off all the idiots in your way, head for the right barrel. You don't need to worry about reining Joe. He will know where to go without you telling him. But, if you want to keep your knees from being ripped off, keep them squeezed as tight as you can against his side."

I nodded, a little worried.

"When he finishes circling the right barrel, he'll circle the left and then the far barrel. At that point, he will straighten up and race to the finish line…the same as the start line here. All you need to do is kick him as hard as you can and give him his head."

I looked out over the course and drew the path in my mind. It seemed easy enough. I urged Joe up to the start line. Mick waited, a look of incredulity on his face.

"What?" I asked.

"You are to be going top speed when you cross the start line. Where do you think you should set up?"

"Not here?" I offered.

He nodded with raised eyebrows. "Holy Mary, what have I gotten myself into?" he muttered.

(Way better language than his usual fare, by the way.)

I turned Joe and trotted a few feet away.

"Further."

"Will they allow that?"

Mick sucked in a deep breath, and I feared what was about to follow.

"I'll back up," I said quickly.

I moved at least thirty feet from the start line.

He rubbed his forehead and waited.

"Am I far enough back?"

"You could not get far enough back from me," he said, in a tired voice.

I ignored the implied insult, and gathered my reins. As ready as I was ever going to be.

"Go!" Mick shouted.

I kicked Joe, and yelled, "Hah!" like I'd seen Mick do a thousand times. Joe's head shot up, but he didn't move. This is not the way I ever treated Joe, and he was baffled.

"Joe, canter," I whispered.

Joe shot forward, and cantered across the start line. He instantly zeroed in on the right barrel. Mick was correct. Joe needed nothing from me except to hang on. I grabbed the saddle horn and hugged my knees tight around Joe. The barrel skimmed against my legs as Joe swirled around it and catapulted to the next one. I was only there for the ride. Joe was on auto-pilot. He whipped around the second barrel, which tottered a bit, and then he was on his way for the third. I could not believe how fast this little horse could go! He rocketed around the last barrel, and then roared to the finish line. He raced past Mick, and kept going, across the yard, and a quarter mile up the trail before I was able to stop him.

Sheepishly, I trotted back to Mick.

"How was that?" I asked.

Mick was on the ground laughing. I am not kidding. Rolling on the ground clutching his stomach, convulsed with laughter. I waited, while Joe blew streams of air from his flared nostrils. After some time, it was apparent that Mick would be laughing for a while, so I turned Joe back to the barn.

I dismounted and led him into the barn. Milly was filling a grain bucket.

"How did the barrel racing practice go?"

"Okay, I guess. I don't think I'm very good."

"Oh?"

Mick came into the barn then, still chuckling. Milly gazed at him for a moment. "Will she be ready in a month?"

"For a total dork, she sure knows how to go. But, I don't know if a month is long enough to teach her how to stop."

I pulled Joe's saddle off and began brushing his back, glancing at Mick. That had sounded dangerously close to a compliment. Joe looked different than usual. He arched his neck and his tail swept back and forth. His normally sleepy expression was replaced by an excited sparkle in his eyes. My old horse had enjoyed that! How I would have loved to have seen the young Joe, in his virile youth.

As I brushed him, Milly moved from stall to stall filling grain bins. Burton and the other workers were already in the pasture, filling the feed bin with hay. Mick began breaking apart hay bales and tossing the sections into the indoor stalls. I finished brushing Joe quickly and led him to the back barn door. He paused as I pulled off his halter.

"See you tomorrow, Joe," I said, kissing his muzzle, "That was fun."

He pulled away as the halter slipped off, and walked carefully across the mud pit. As soon as he'd cleared that booby trap, he shook his head and cantered away. I watched as he disappeared over a dip in the field.

The other horses lifted their heads as he whirled past them. One or two nickered, and trotted briefly, as though to follow him, then thought better of it. With the promise of spring trickling like sap through his veins, my old horse scampered, remembering his youth.

Chapter Nineteen

Amy had been practicing quite a bit on little Nipper. At age ten, she was eager to join the trail rides, especially since her big sister had been promoted to a trail guide. I guess Milly felt that Amy had enough skill to be the follower, and as spring arrived and the trail rides started back up, Amy was finally given the go-ahead to take Nipper as the follower.

This would be Nipper's first trail ride since becoming a one-eyed pony. If I felt any concern over this, or protective instincts towards my little sister, I don't remember them. After all, when I had started at the farm and was only nine, I had never ridden a horse when I was sent off on *my* first trail ride. Surely Amy at age *ten* would be fine, even if her pony did only have one eye.

The trail horses were saddled. I often saddled Joe now, so that he would become increasingly comfortable under saddle. He never seemed to be the slightest concerned about me riding him in the saddle. However, when Mick once approached him with the saddle, he kicked a fierce hoof at Mick. Mick backed away, and that was the last time Mick ever tried to go near Joe that I can remember.

The trail riders were hoisted onto their horses, and we ambled along to the trail head, single file. Amy, on little one-eyed Nipper, brought up the rear. It was a wonderful day, and such a delight to have me and Amy in charge of all those horses!

It started off just fine. There was no portent of disaster…yet. Robins were winging, birds were singing, trees were budding. The sun was shining and all was right with the world. *Almost*. Nipper was clearly not quite used to seeing the world with one eye. He seemed a little agitated by the sounds coming from the blind side. We were out perhaps about a mile when disaster struck.

An old Christmas tree with fluttering tinsel had been tossed along the side of the trail. Joe glanced at it, and huffed, but moved on without more than a glance. The lazy old trail horses noticed it too. They also gave it a quick look, and passed by. Then one-eyed Nipper came upon the Christmas tree. A breeze fluttered the tinsel. The pony saw the sparkle and fluttering out of the corner of his good eye, and knew that death was imminent. With a frenzied snort, he took off at a gallop. Amy, to her credit, hung on. Nipper first ran almost into the heels of the horse in front of him, alerting the group that disaster was at hand and every one of them better make a dash for it. Every horse, even my dependable Joe, leaped after the one-eyed pony. With Nipper leading the way, they all turned back to the barn at a thunderous gallop, retracing the steps we had so calmly traversed but a few brief moments ago.

I feared that I had lost control. So much for feeling smug about me and Amy being in charge. We were about as *in charge* as the village of Pompeii when Vesuvius erupted.

The whole pack was in a stampede back to the barn. You have got to give little one-eyed Nipper credit. How those tiny little legs managed to outrun all the horses was a marvel.

I found myself clinging to the saddle horn, grateful I had saddled Joe that day. Like I have mentioned before, I was a much better rider than I was a year ago, but no one would dare call me an accomplished rider. And Joe's gallop was not a whole lot easier to sit than his trot. I was bouncing around at least hard enough to cause brain damage. *If I survived.*

Unfortunately, I had two years more riding experience than everyone else on that trail. It would have been actually quite hilarious to replay in slow motion the facial expressions and riding techniques of that crew as they thundered back towards the barn. It was like every one of them was watching the Exorcist for the first time. There was at least that much terror written across every face.

I hoped beyond hope that no one would be killed. I had no idea how I was going to explain to my mother the certain maiming and trampling of Amy who still clung (barely) to Nipper's back. Mom may have practiced Benign Neglect, but I bet she would not be charitable to *me* for practicing it. Or Milly. I think major law suits were not out of the question.

I still held out hope that the horses would gather their wits and calm down before we came into Milly's sight. However, it seemed far-fetched given the degree of white visible in every eye. I was not optimistic this was going to end well.

I can't imagine what was going through Amy's head at this point. Here she was, ten-years-old, on a one-eyed pony that had decided tinsel was a mortal enemy. On top of that, he knew that if he slowed down, his little pony bones were going to be crushed by a bunch of senile, panicked horses. He was running for dear life, and he could only see half of his visual field.

Amy could see none, because her eyes were tightly clenched shut. However, when she peeked, she noticed the barn coming at her at an alarming rate. Little one-eyed Nipper was going to race into the door of the barn and there was no doubt, that Amy was going to be smacked right off his back by the door jamb as surely as the trail riders were going to ask for their money back.

While Amy was anticipating her next move, which was likely her last, there were brewing troubles behind her. One of the more precariously seated riders finally lost his war with inertia, and flew off his horse. His forehead had an unfortunate, really rather *devastating* encounter with a tree trunk. I would gladly have stopped to help him, but Joe had no interest in stopping yet.

Horrors were not yet over. There, before us, stood Milly, mouth agape, and disbelief on her face. To be fair…what did she expect? I was twelve-years-old, edging on thirteen, and Amy was barely ten. And yet, Milly had put us in charge of some 20,000 pounds of horse-flesh. I don't think we weighed more than 150 pounds between us.

Amy made an executive decision. It was die by trampling or die by crushing her skull against the top of the door. She toppled off of Nipper. Nipper did indeed barrel through the door, sans Amy, and I presume he crashed into some wall.

Amy curled up in fetal position and awaited her crushed skull. The rest of the herd scattered all about the yard, coming eventually to a stop. They all milled by the fence, huffing and snorting, while the fallen rider stumbled toward Milly, forehead dripping blood.

I had a sneaky suspicion I was in trouble.

Milly was ominously quiet as she helped each rider down off their horse and promised them a refund or a rain check on a future ride. Can you believe not a single person took the rain check?

Amy escaped without even one broken bone. Thank the Lord for little favors! I quickly blamed Amy, and Milly looked at me with disappointment. I don't remember letting Milly down often, but I had definitely failed her this time.

My mother never heard about this particular adventure. The only thing in fact that she remembers about either me or Amy at the farm is that I was never home. I practically lived at the farm. And she remembers that I got worms.

Mom was remembering the worm debacle correctly. I *did* get pinworms and that was a terrifying experience. Almost every kid at the farm ended up getting worms at one time or another. But Mom says that she does not remember us encountering *any* other dangers from the farm or "surely I wouldn't have let you go there."

Vicky Kaseorg

Chapter Twenty

My sister Wendy visited the farm once with my baby sister, Holly. As she put it, *You deal with the horse, and I'll take pictures.* Holly was an adorable little thing and about one-year-old when Wendy brought her to see the horses.

Wendy herself was afraid of the horses. Like I said before, she did not like animals, except cats. I considered that a fatal flaw and just another good reason to claw her to death if I had the opportunity. However, no one else was offering to take pictures of my beloved Joe. I guess Wendy had a heart somewhere. She just kept it well hidden from me, usually.

I brushed Joe thoroughly, so he would be beautiful for the photo shoot.

"You can't brush away ugly," Mick said, walking by with a pitchfork in hand. He was always grumpy when assigned to stall cleaning duty. I had finished my set of stalls already.

I kept brushing Joe, turning a deaf ear to Mick. He kicked at a cat that was in his path. My goodness! Foul mood today! Must be Debby was home brushing her teeth and would be in late. Must take her hours to brush those tusks.

"Milly," I said when she walked in, "My sister is coming in a few minutes. I was going to take Joe to the trail behind the barn for some pictures. Is that okay?"

"He'll break the camera!" Mick shouted from the stall, "Unless it focuses on your face first. Then *you'll* break the camera."

"Mick," Milly growled, "That was uncalled for."

"The truth hurts," he mumbled.

"So will the belt," Burton roared, who happened to be on his way to a rare visit with the stallion. We were all warned to stay out of the yard while Burton walked the stallion to a back field. I had never seen the stallion, though I had heard him in his self-appointed demolition of his shed many times.

"Everyone stay in the barn," Burton ordered, and strode out the door with the cruelest looking halter I had ever seen. It had a metal choke chain that could tighten around the horse's muzzle. None of us kids would ever dare defy Burton, but we all crept to the door and peered out. Even Mick leaned on the stall door, poking his head out the window.

There was an enormous amount of banging and possible wood splitting, then a few choice words and some roars. We all cringed. The shed door slammed open and out walked a prancing, snorting, devil himself in a horse suit. He would have trampled anyone else but Burton for sure. I would have been a pancake within three seconds. Burton had the chain tightly clamped around the stallion's muzzle and his hand was right beneath the horse's chin. He jerked the chain repeatedly. The horse flung his head as much as he was able, but it was clear the chain hurt him. He danced on his dangerous hooves, kicking out every few steps. Somehow Burton managed to stay with him, and a shaking teen opened a gate into the pasture. The teen slammed it shut, then wiped his forehead. He'd been at the very gate of hell and survived.

We all poked our head out the door, and watched as Burton continued wrestling with the stallion, leading him to one of the furthest fields, that had its own gated section.

Finally, he shoved the horse through the gate, while pulling off the halter. The horse lunged at him with vicious teeth, at least as big as Debby's. Burton smacked him brutally with the halter, and the horse wheeled away. It galloped across the field with a triumphant neighing.

"Why does he keep that horse?" I asked.

"The ladies love him," Mick said, returning to his work. The kids dispersed to their various chores. I went to the tack room for Joe's hackamore, and slid it over his nose. Unhooking him from the wall ring, I stroked his face.

"Ready to meet my sister?"

Milly glanced over. "Have fun."

I nodded and led my shining pony out to the riding ring. I jumped onto his back, pulling myself up with his mane, still terribly clumsy in mounting the horses. Fortunately, Mick was nowhere in sight or I would have gotten the usual string of abuse.

I practiced trying to sit his jiggly trot, with about as much success as usual, and then urged him into a canter. One of the things that Joe always got right was cantering on the correct lead. That would matter in the Western Pleasure class at the upcoming show, and it was what helped him to be so well-balanced in the barrel races. When a horse canters around the ring, the leg furthest from the fence, or inside the turn, is the one that leads the stride. For my first show when I won first place on Rockabye, I didn't even know about leads. Now I did, but I never had to ask Joe to take the correct lead. He always did.

The rider's equitation or riding skill was not specifically judged in Western Pleasure. In general, the slow, calm and controlled gaits and demeanor of the horse was judged. The horse was to be a "pleasure" to ride, hence the name. However, a rider that kept a nice, balanced position certainly aided the horse in the smoothness of his gaits. Poor Joe was going to have to contend with a rider that looked like she was on a pogo stick during the trot. I just was not having much success melting into the saddle as Milly had advised.

I almost always wore my hair in two ponytails, rubber-banded above my ears. They flopped up and down like bird wings during the trot, bringing special attention to how poor my seat was. I might want to create a different hairdo for the show.

In the distance, Wendy carried baby Holly, approaching the farm. Wendy was like Holly's second mother. This was good since Benign Neglect of one-year-olds is most successful with a lot of back-up help. Wendy was very loving to Holly, in sharp contrast to her treatment of me.

I urged Joe out of the ring, and we greeted Wendy and baby Holly, just as Burton was returning from the field.

"Who's this?" he asked.

"These are my sisters, Wendy and Holly," I said.

"Pleased to meet you," Burton said, with a blast of gentility I had never heard from him before. He noticed Wendy's camera.

"Here to take some pictures?"

"Yes, of Holly on the horse with Vicky."

Burton blinked, and looked at me.

"What's wrong? You don't like your baby sister?"

Wendy looked a little worried.

"Is it safe?"

"Hell no," laughed Burton.

He tipped his head and then strode away. I know I use that word a lot for Burton, but he had legs about two miles long. He was always striding. What else could such long legs do?

"Is he serious?" Wendy asked, the little mother hen.

"No, Joe is perfectly safe. Does he look dangerous?"

Joe gazed at Wendy with his gentle, brown eyes. He stood quietly, facing her. Baby Holly was not quite sure what to think of Joe. The only animal she'd ever seen was Lady, our dog.

"Puppy!" she said finally.

"Horse," Wendy corrected her, "Dangerous horse."

"He's not dangerous. Pet his muzzle."

She shook her head, laughing nervously.

"Oh no, not me. You handle the horses and I'll take the pictures."

"He won't bite you."

"Then we are even. I won't bite him. But I won't pet him either. You got worms from these horses."

"No I didn't. I got worms from the dirt. Pinworms live in the dirt."

"Well horses roll in dirt. I'll just take pictures. You pet the horses and you get the worms."

I sighed. Thank God Mick wasn't around to hear that discussion. That was all I needed, broadcasting the news of my worms, which were gone by this time. The icky tasting medicine washes them right out of you.

"Let's keep it down about the worms, ok?"

Wendy followed my glance to Mick and the wheelbarrow across the yard. "Gotcha," she said with a grin, "Mums the worm...I mean word."

Wendy was funny, I have to give her that. But she was a big fat chicken too. For her to hand Holly up to me, she had to get close to Joe.

"He's awfully big," she complained.

"No, he's not. He's not even a horse. He's a pony."

"What if he steps on me?"

"He won't. Just come up beside me and hand me Holly."

Finally, after some inch by inch sidling closer, she handed the baby to me, and backed away quickly.

"Puppy!" Holly said, patting Joe's neck.

We started down the trail with Holly happily whacking Joe's neck. She didn't seem at all frightened. Wendy, however, continued to keep her distance.

"Turn around!" she called. I steered Joe back down the trail towards Wendy while she took pictures. She moved a little closer to get a close-up of Holly.

"Horsy, Holly," I told her.

"Horse," she mimicked, "Woof, woof."

"No, a horse says, neigh."

I tried to neigh like a horse and Joe swiveled his ears back.

He was not angry. He was just listening. I knew Joe's moods as well as my own by now. I could tell just by looking at his expression how he was feeling. I knew when Mick was coming before anyone else, just by watching Joe. Joe never liked Mick.

"Let's get some pictures of Joe alone now," Wendy suggested. For someone who hated me and hated animals, she was being pretty nice. I thought maybe she was up to something, but I was delighted to get pictures of my horse.

"You have to take Holly before I can get off," I told her.

"Does that mean I have to come close?"

"Unless you want me to throw Holly to you."

"How good is your aim?"

"Wendy, just come get the baby."

Wendy finally tiptoed close enough for me to hand off Holly and I dismounted. We took a few more photos, a close up of Joe's face and a side shot.

"Do all horses have such big bellies?" Wendy asked, "And such a big curve in their back?"

Poor Joe. Could no one look beyond the minor defects to see the inner beauty? Not even my sister who had probably never even approached a live horse before in her life?

"Not all," I said.

"Pretty!" said Holly, playing in the dirt, and stuffing some in her mouth.

I didn't think eating Burton's Farm dirt was a good idea but Holly was happy, and Wendy had to put her down for the pictures.

"Yes, he's pretty," I told Holly.

"Those other horses look kinda scruffy," said Wendy, pointing to the trail horses who had gathered along the fence behind us.

I looked over at the horses. I knew of course that Burton's horses were not pure-bred prizes by any stretch of the imagination, but I never thought of them as ugly. They were horses, and horses are beautiful.

"They still have their winter coats."

"But it's June."

Now June may be summer in most parts of the country but Chicago has been known to have snow still in May, and even in June. Winter in Chicago is nothing like the winters we had in Memphis.

I pointed that out to Wendy who had finished her picture taking and now with a screech, noticed Holly was chowing down on dirt like it was chocolate pudding. She snatched the baby, and wiped as much mud as she could away from Holly's cute little mouth.

"Well, is there anything else we should see while we're here?" she asked.

"Do you want to see the cow that thinks she's a bull?"

Wendy was not interested in that, but she liked the goats, and the cute baby chickens which skittered about the yard. Holly called everything *puppy*, but she learned quickly when we corrected her. Zeke erupted in snarls and dreadful growling and barking as we passed the shed he was tied to. He was an equal opportunity killer – he'd have as quickly eaten cute baby Holly as grizzled Milly.

I shared Wendy's worried look as we hurried past Zeke, back to the ring, where I had tied Joe.

"Puppy!" said Holly as we left Zeke behind, "Nice puppy."

Joe was napping, as the sun stretched across his back.

"Do you want to get on him?" I asked Wendy.

"Oh noooooo."

I climbed back on Joe after untying him from the fence.

"Here, hand me Holly, and I'll carry her back to the road for you."

Wendy handed my little sister up to me, and I urged Joe forward. She trailed us as Joe broke into a trot. I kept one arm tightly around Holly as we both bounced up and down on Joe's bone-crunching trot.

Holly found this very funny, and laughed with delight. Joe's ears flicked back and forth. His trot seemed to smooth out. It may have been my imagination, but it sure felt like Joe was trying to be careful, as though he knew he carried precious cargo on his back. I know that couldn't be possible, but it sure appeared that way to me.

Chapter Twenty-One

The 4-H show was upon us. The first thing I did was panic. After that, I called upon my talisman. When we lived in Memphis, I found a little gold key chain in a creek across the street from our house. On the front of a little circle attached to the keychain was an engraving of hands praying. On the back was the "Serenity Prayer."

Lord, grant me the serenity

To accept the things I cannot change.

The courage to change the things I can.

And the wisdom to know the difference.

Amen.

I knew God was speaking directly to me through the keychain. I named the keychain Goldie, because of the incredibly clever perception that it was gold colored. I spent many hours with Goldie in my pocket, memorizing the verse and contemplating the message.

Whenever I went through stressful times in life, I pulled Goldie out of my pocket, and tried to think "What would Goldie do?" It is remarkable how often the simple prayer on the back of Goldie guided me through a complicated mess of trauma and trouble.

As I dressed for the 4-H show, I put Goldie on my bed and reread the verse. I thought carefully about each line, trying not to hyperventilate. I was a nervous child, and had great anxiety when forced to perform in front of others. How on earth was I going to do three horse classes with people watching me? I still couldn't sit a trot, any number of disasters could occur with a cart, and barrel racing was downright dangerous.

Goldie shimmered on my bed.

I read the first line: *God grant me the serenity to accept the things I cannot change.*

Okay. Lucky for me, my parents spoke in multi-syllables and I knew what serenity meant. Peace. Calmness. All I wasn't feeling at the moment.

Accept what I cannot change.

Well, I have paid my money, and I am registered. The show is today, and Milly is probably pulling the trailer into position as we speak. I cannot change any of this, so I need to be cool. What's done is done. I am going to the 4-H show with Joe and I am in three classes. Move on.

Next line: *The courage to change the things I can.*

What can I change? I can change freaking out about this. I can choose to remain calm. I can change my shirt because this one has a stain. I can change caring whether I win a blue ribbon or not. I can change whether I choose to let a poor showing define me as a despicable human being that no one should love. Yes. I can change my response to whatever happens. I can't control the judges or the verdicts…but I can control whether I let it deflate me. Maybe. At least I can try.

Next line: *And the wisdom to know the difference. Amen.*

Now that's a tough one. Let's see. I can't change Joe's trot. He is going to bounce me to Kingdom Come no matter what I do. So it is wise to accept this limitation. I am going to bounce because I am on a bouncy horse. Can I change the judge's perception? Maybe. If I look like I am supposed to be bouncing on the bouncy trot, they may give me a pass. If I smile and look like I am not smashing my brain against my skull and causing neurological trauma, they might not notice. Wisdom, wisdom, wisdom.

Wisdom to know the difference. The more I thought about that, the more I forgot about the 4-H show, and contemplated the horse I was about to enter the show upon. A year ago, Joe was hated by everyone, and no one could ride him. He wouldn't let a saddle within a mile of him, and Milly wondered how they could afford to keep him. Now, a one-year-old child had whomped him repeatedly while riding on his back and he hadn't flinched. A terrible rider (yours truly) could not only come near him with a saddle, but tighten the cinch, hop on, and ride him anywhere she wanted without so much as an irritated snort. Mick still hated Joe, and maybe Burton did too, but Milly, and me, and bunches of the teens now stopped to pet him, and notice what a nice horse Joe had become.

Many things had changed because a little stupid girl had the wisdom to know they *could* be changed. Maybe I wasn't so hopeless after all.

I put Goldie back in her special silver box, and hurried out the door.

"Bye, Mom!"

My folks just thought it was another day of Vicky at the farm. They didn't even know I was in three classes at the 4-H horse show. Sometimes Benign Neglect is taken a bit far, in my opinion, but I had the *serenity to accept the things I cannot change.*

I ran to the farm. Once I made up my mind that I was going to go, do my best, and have the wisdom to know the difference of what I could change, and what I could not, I couldn't wait to get there.

We all clambered into Milly's van while Burton drove the trailer with the horses. We arrived, and unloaded the horses. My first class was Western Pleasure Ponies. Since Joe was under 14.2 hands, he was classified as a pony. I was twelve at the time, so one of the older kids on a pony. I was competing against kids as young as eight-years-old. This was a little embarrassing and Mick, who went along for the ride and to cheer Debby on, was sure to use that fact to full advantage. Thank the Lord, puny Peeper opted to ride in different classes than mine. There is no doubt she would have creamed me. The Barrel Race Ponies followed a few classes after Pleasure. Then I had a long break, and my final class was the Pleasure Pony Driving.

Fortunately, I was not in direct competition with Debby in any class since Rockabye was a horse, not a pony. I did discover that this 4-H contest was run a little differently than the last one. The top ten places were awarded ribbons, first to tenth place. I was not guaranteed a ribbon like I had been in my class with Thumper and Lady.

My Western Pleasure class was one of the first classes, so I saddled and bridled Joe, and took him to an outer practice ring to warm up. Some of the requirements judges look for are loose reins, slow controlled gaits, and a calm horse. Joe was usually good in all those areas, but there was one area I had a little bit of lip chewing over. Joe did not like other horses, and at the end of the class, the horses were required to line up in the center of the ring, one right next to each other. I just wasn't sure if Joe would do that without taking out a few of the other ponies. That would certainly decrease my chances of a ribbon.

The class was large, and filled with ponies ridden by little people. I felt conspicuous as one of the older kids. I noticed Mick along the ring as I entered, with my reins loose at a walk. I kept a good distance behind the pony in front of me since Joe was already showing signs of discontent with the proximity of other members of his species. Debby wasn't with Mick since her class was shortly after mine, Western Pleasure Horse. I tried not to glance at Mick, but really couldn't help it. He was making a baby rocking motion with his arms, and sucking his thumb, then pointing at me. I tried to keep my eyes on the tail in front of me.

So did Joe. At one point, Joe snapped back his ears, and lunged at a pony passing us. Fortunately, the judge wasn't looking. That pony did not have an unhurried walk. In fact, he broke into a trot. The judges did glance over then, but Joe had already settled down again, and I was pretty sure that was my mulligan.

The judge told us to trot. Joe knew voice commands, and he instantly began trotting. He was so instant in fact that he almost plowed into the pony in front of us. I passed and circled across the ring. It seemed it would be wise to find another pony to trail. The judge smiled at me, so I hoped that maneuver didn't disqualify me. He may have been smiling at all the daylight he saw between my bottom and the saddle, but I chose to consider it a smile of encouragement.

"Lope."

I never used the word lope with Joe. It is a more sedate canter. I had to squeeze Joe's sides to urge him to "lope" which was good because he didn't obey so quickly that he crashed into the pony ahead of us. He was perfect in his lope, and perfect in the correct lead leg. Still, he was bigger than most of the ponies, and so I had to circle across the ring again. Finding a clear spot to lope was the only chance I had of preventing an assault by my pleasure pony on slower victims.

Then we walked, and were told to come to the center of the ring. Oh-oh. Here is was. The moment of truth. Joe's ears were already swiveling as ponies crowded in. I made a quick decision and steered him towards the end of the line-up. Our only chance at survival was not to be hemmed in on both sides. Fortunately, no one else had the same thought and I snagged the coveted end position.

Then the judge came one by one to each pony. He stopped in front of each, looking us over, taking some notes, and then asking us to back up.

Back up? I knew Joe could do that, but I had never really practiced it. There were rarely good reasons to go backwards…not on a horse, and not in life.

Still, the judge worked his way down the line, and Joe had his ears perked, watching all the ponies beside him backing up. I have always felt Joe was an exceptionally smart horse, and I could see his wheels turning. He was taking it all in, and figuring out that the next duty was to go backwards.

The judge stopped in front of me. He looked us over as I tried to sit calmly, as though filled with pleasure. I knew the point of Western Pleasure riding was to have horse and rider have a *calm, pleasurable demeanor* and so I was doing my best to evoke *pleasure*. I slouched a little so I didn't look too uptight, and pasted a fake smile on my face. The reins were slack and my pony was relaxed. Well, except for the ears flicking back as the judge came near. Joe wouldn't bite the judge, would he?

"Back up," the judge ordered.

I complied quickly, before Joe decided he could not restrain his inner demons any longer. I pulled back on the reins, squeezing my legs against his sides.

To my relief, and surprise, he backed up a few feet. The judge moved away and told me to return to my place.

That was it. Now we all sat there waiting to see who would go home in shame, and who would go home in victory. The announcer started at tenth place. When he didn't call my name, I deflated a little. I knew I was not among the best out there, but I thought I had had a shot at tenth. I was feeling a little bummed, and started day-dreaming about my next class. I had not practiced nearly enough Barrel Racing, mostly because it scared me to death. Besides that, I could tell Mick thought I was hopeless and he didn't spend much time helping me after that first day.

I was so absorbed in my worries, that I didn't hear the judge when he announced, "Sixth Place, Vicky and Joe." The lady with the ribbons stood waiting, and when I made no move to accept my unexpected reward, she came to me.

"Congratulations," she said, handing me the ribbon.

Joe perked his ears forward. He'd been paying attention and I don't think he was surprised. I glanced at the fence to see if Mick had seen my moment of triumph. He was no longer there. He was probably off helping Daunting Dental get Rockabye ready.

The crowd cheered as the first place winner was pinned, and then all us top ten riders got to do a victory lap. Joe did snap at the fifth place pony, but I don't think it was sour grapes. I hurried from the ring in case the judges were thinking of revoking my prize.

I didn't even bring Joe back to his stall. There were only four classes before my barrel racing class. So I stayed nearby and watched Debby's class walk in. Rockabye was, as always, perfect. Debby didn't have to do a thing but dial in first place. Which she got. But I wasn't jealous.

Barrel Racing was a blur. Joe was the third pony in the class of about twenty entrants. Both Debby and Mick were at the fence watching this one. I was freaking out a little bit, and couldn't remember if I was supposed to go to the left or right barrel first. Then I was lined up at the start, and the announcer said, "Go." I don't think I gave a single command. Joe was off like a shot and all I did was hang on for dear life. I am honestly not sure I even held on to the reins. I think I gripped the saddle horn and closed my eyes. Before I knew what had happened, he had screeched around the three barrels and then galloped to the finish. I had the sense to rein him to a stop before crushing the little 4-H'ers milling about.

I walked him in an adjoining ring to cool him down while the other ponies finished the class. Then we were all called back in for the ribbon ceremony. I was alert for this one. I had no idea how we had done, but Joe is a very good barrel racer, despite his rider. He won fifth! I noticed even Mick and Debby clapped as I grabbed my ribbon from the judge. It might have been because Milly was there too, having materialized out of nowhere. She probably threatened Mick to be nice.

I had plenty of time now to brush Joe, wander the fairgrounds a little, and eat a hotdog while meandering among the animal exhibits. Mostly, I hung out near Joe. Debby came over since Rockabye was stabled nearby.

"Congratulations," she said, as she grabbed a brush and began brushing him.

I looked up, wondering who she was talking to. Mick was nowhere in sight which is probably why she decided to talk to me at all. Still, it was nice of her.

"Thanks. You too."

"Rockabye makes it easy," she admitted.

He sure does. Debby didn't even need to be there, frankly. Rockabye could have won it all on his own with his eyes closed. To my credit, I didn't say that out loud. I didn't even mention that her teeth probably frightened the competition.

Milly appeared now and offered to help me get the cart and harness ready. My last class had arrived. There were only ten ponies in this class. Milly flicked her long braid to her back, and told me I had done a great job on Joe so far. I nodded, and smiled. As we lined up for the class, I noticed right away that the other ponies had fancy harnesses and shiny new carts. Joe's cart was faded, chipped, worn, and old. The harness was cracked with weathered leather that had seen better days, probably a century ago. I felt distinctly out-classed. Joe didn't seem to care. He shook his head proudly, his long mane beautifully combed and tangle free. He could have been the star of a Breck Shampoo commercial.

Milly led him to the ring while I sat feeling miserable in the cart. I had rubbed off all the cobwebs, but there was no hiding the fact that our cart was as dilapidated as everything at Burton's Farm.

"Be proud," whispered Milly, as the drivers were called into the ring.

This was a harrowing class, perhaps even more so than the barrel racing. One little pony went a little crazy and began cantering around the ring. The little girl who was driving the cart looked terrified, and clearly had no idea of what to do. A few of the other horses spooked and carts were rolling every which way. I kept Joe on the edge of the ring, and he shook his head, but stayed at a walk. The wild pony was finally caught, and the now sobbing driver, with her naughty pony and cart led out of the ring.

One less pony meant I was that much closer to a ribbon. I didn't feel a bit sorry for the little girl. The rest of the class was much calmer. Joe did his best, and there were no further mishaps. It took me a while to maneuver Joe to get our cart to the center of the ring when the class ended. The judge did notice that. Drat.

The wild pony was disqualified, so there were only nine ribbons to be awarded. I just didn't want to be ninth. I would never hear the end of it. Besides, I felt protective of Burton's Farm, and I knew our cart was a little embarrassing. However, this class wasn't about the cart. It was about how well the pony was in control and listened to the driver's commands. Joe was a great cart pony. He didn't deserve last place.

I held my breath. Yay! Ninth place went to a shiny black cart with red ribbons entwined along its polished seat. They matched the ribbons in the horse's tail. How I wished I'd thought to bedeck Joe in ribbons!

Eighth place. Still not me.

Seventh place. Nope, not me. That honor went to a cream colored cart with sky blue cushions drawn by a cream colored pony. Gag me with a spoon.

Sixth place? Not Joe. Sixth place was a beautiful deep bay colored pony with tricolored ribbons in his mane that matched the tri-colored spokes on the cart wheels. Over the top for 4-H if you ask me.

Fifth place? No! I had just topped my best performance. I didn't even notice what driver won fifth place. Here's where I must step momentarily out of the past. Fifty years later, I have clear recollections of winning the Driving Class. However, the only other ribbon I have found in my old scrapbooks is a fourth place ribbon. Now I am thrilled with fourth place, but I wonder why I have such a clear recollection of first place.

I know that what the judges saw was an ugly horse with an ugly cart. They probably could not have given me first place even if they wanted. However, I know what Joe had been, and what he had become. In my mind, I gave him the award he deserved, and fifty years later, that's what I remembered. He won first place.

Chapter Twenty-Two

Ah! The lazy, hazy days of summer. My little sister, Amy hadn't been at the farm much over the winter and early spring. Milly always said you could tell when spring returned for good when Amy returned to the farm. Amy loved the horses, but not with quite the same ferocity as I did. She was a fair-weather farm-hand.

I didn't blame her. Winters in Chicago were brutal. The lake effect snow from Lake Michigan guaranteed that several feet of snow often pummeled us. It was a lot of fun, but bitter cold. I don't know how I managed to plow my way to the farm through the enormous drifts that often lined the streets. Not a few times I got nearly buried by a passing snow plow spewing the contents from the streets onto the narrow path by the busy highway.

So, I was happy when summer arrived for several reasons. No more braving snow drifts taller than me. Even better, school was out, and I was free for endless days at the farm. The disadvantage of summer is that the piles of manure thawed, and with it, the frozen smell molecules. I don't know if this is scientifically accurate, but there is no doubt that summer brought out the worst of the manure odors. And flies. I know the old adage is flies to honey, but honey has *nothing* on manure in attracting flies.

The huge manure pile was a towering Mount Olympus. Burton decided it was time for the semi-annual manure repositioning. Manure never left the farm. It just got moved around. Horses moved it from their guts to the stalls. We moved it from the stalls to the manure mountain. Burton moved it from the manure mountain to other locations on the farm. You know energy is never created nor destroyed. Same with manure. It just changes addresses.

Burton had a small front-end loader, decrepit as everything else on the farm. The horses were closed off in a back pasture and the massive gates into the field from the yard swung open. Then with an ear shattering rumble, the old loader chugged across the hard packed dirt. We kids were lined up on the hay bales watching. Burton lowered the giant shovel of the loader, and rammed it into the edge of the immense pile. As the rusty shovel dug into the imposing mess of poop, it released a whole new category of stench. Steam rose from the decomposing mess. Then Burton swiveled the growling machine around and headed out to the field where the manure was deposited along the edge of a distant fence. I wondered how he managed to be downwind of that and remain conscious.

That wasn't the only fate for the pile of manure, however. People would actually come to cart barrels of it away, and pay Burton for the privilege! It was great fertilizer, and master gardeners loved it. That always amazed me. I could think of at least a thousand ways I'd rather spend money.

This seems a good place to mention how I *did* spend money. Every spare cent I got went towards horse statues. I probably had thousands of them. Most of them were cheap plastic things that were clumsily constructed, but a few of them were really special. My favorite was one that Dad gave me for Christmas. It was made of real horsehair. It is pretty clear I didn't ponder very long how that statue was made, or I would have been horrified. However, I loved my real horsehair statue, oblivious to the fact that it was in reality dead horse hide. My next favorite horse statues comprised a family of light brown horses with black manes. There was a stallion, a mare, and a little filly. I played for hours with those horse statues. My little horse family all had names, and personalities. I enacted many heart-wrenching dramas with that little family. They were very important to me, and slept in the little shelves at the head of my bed. They had many harrowing adventures at the whim of my imagination, but that little family always emerged intact. My little horse family stood firm against the world.

Meanwhile, back to the farm. By now, I was a seasoned trail guide at the ripe old age of twelve going on thirteen. Amy, at age ten, had even been allowed to lead trails on little one-eyed Nipper. That she survived, and that the trail riders survived is proof positive that angels watch over children. It was lunacy to put little Amy on a one-eyed pony in charge of *anything*, let alone a lineup of 20,000 pounds of horseflesh and incompetent riders.

There were trails every hour throughout the morning and afternoon of the summer. Weekends were always swamped with trail rides. Summer was the farm's season to make enough money to survive another year, so the poor horses went on way more trail rides than they wanted, or should have been. All of us were weary by the end of the day. Still, I never complained. I was exhausted, but it was an elated exhaustion. Mick tried to get out of leading the trails whenever possible. Mostly he did so by pawning it off on me. Despite his continual verbal abuse, I was still hopelessly in love with him, and thought if I took over his trails, maybe he would insult me less. (It didn't work.) It wasn't a huge sacrifice, since I loved every opportunity I could get to ride. However, even I grew weary of being a trail-guide by my fourth or fifth trail of the day.

So when the opportunity for different experiences came up, I jumped at them. The kids were offered small payment for helping with "pony parties." This is where parents set up birthday parties for their kids, and hired Burton's Farm to show up with ponies. We workers helped load the ponies in the horse trailer, brushed and tacked them, and then led the ponies in circles around the back-yard of the customer. It wasn't a lot of money for the workers, but it was a change of scenery. It was a good source of income for the farm, however, and they booked them as often as possible.

By now, Joe was so comfortable under saddle that Milly asked me what I thought of using Joe at a pony party. I thought we ought to try him out with a rider other than me on the saddle before we endangered the life of some stranger's precious little five-year-old.

Yeah…I know. Strange that the twelve-year-old me suggested that safety precaution to the responsible adult.

Now Joe had been fine with me and baby Holly on his back, but how would he be with a total stranger alone on his back? Up to this point, no one ever rode Joe in a saddle except me. So, we used Peeper for our practice rider. She was not afraid of anything and a willing victim.

I saddled Joe, and held onto the hackamore reins while Milly placed Peeper on the saddle. Joe lazily closed his eyes.

"I don't think it will be a problem," I said.

"Lead him around," Milly suggested.

So I walked Joe around the yard and he followed placidly. His healing seemed complete, at least as long as I was nearby. Milly didn't bring Joe to pony parties without me, but when I was able to go, he became a productive income-producing member of the farm, at last.

The little kids loved Joe. For one thing, he was the biggest pony. Everyone wanted to ride him. He was remarkably patient with the children, as though he recognized the need to be calm and gentle. They sometimes bounced about on the saddle, tugged hard at his mane, or patted his neck a little too vigorously, but he never became even remotely riled. He was a great party pony. Amy tagged along to the pony parties, leading little one-eyed Nipper.

Sometimes in the summer, my parents let me go back to the farm after dinner. It was a magical place in the early evening. As the light diffused and turned shades of golden red, and shadows lengthened, one almost didn't notice the patches of raw wood poking through fading paint, or the broken slats in the fence, or the patches of weeds and mud instead of grass. As the sun dipped lower, shooting arcs of red and orange across the deepening blue sky, with the horses' dark silhouettes on the fields, it was beautiful.

A hush always settled over the farm after the animals were fed, and the work was done, and the day was drawing to a close. We would all sit on the hay bales watching the sun set as the fireflies emerged. Even Mick was somewhat companionable then, all of us in a line, guzzling our cans of pop.

Burton joined us at times, telling bawdy jokes. Milly shook her head, and rolled her eyes, but she smiled at him in a way that told me she loved him. Most of the time, however, it was just us kids. Milly and Burton disappeared frequently, leaving us all alone. That suited me fine.

One evening, as I often did, I slipped away from the others and headed out to the peaceful pasture. The horses were grazing on the few sparse tufts of grass they could find. Joe lounged where he almost always stood -- by the pond, near the crab-apple tree.

I loved seeing him with his head low, one leg bent and hoof tilted on its tip, eyes closed. He was an old horse, and tired by the end of a long day of trails. As the sun cast its magenta rays on his back, I clicked my tongue as I approached, and his head swung up.

He always looked happy to see me, even when I interrupted his nap. I gave him a carrot, and then swung myself on his back. Laying down across his withers I hugged my arms around his chest, feeling the warm sun-drenched heat of him soaking into my skin. He stood still as I watched the sun set from my favorite perch on earth. Just as the sun dipped to the horizon, sheets of greenish and white lights spread in waves across the sky.

I had studied aurora borealis in school, and knew I was being given a rare glimpse of one of the prettiest of heaven's displays. Joe lifted his head and looked for all the world like he was watching too. Soon, the lights subsided and the darkness began to fall across the quiet fields.

I slipped off my horse's back and nestled his muzzle in my hands, giving him the last carrot, tucked deep in my pocket.

"See you tomorrow, old friend." He watched me jog back across the field, scramble over the fence and wave to the kids still seated on the hay bales.

"What's your hurry?" Mick asked, "They already ran out of the *pretty* faces."

"Lucky for you they got in a special order of stupid." I *did* say that. Not to his face, of course…not until I was half way home and finally came up with it. *Then,* I said it out loud. I thought it was a really great line.

Chapter Twenty-Three

Alas, like all good things, summer came to an end. Seventh grade commenced and I fell in love with the Bava Brothers. They were twins, Mike and Mark Bava. I couldn't tell them apart, so I loved both of them. This is not to say that I lost my hopeless, undying love for Mick. I would always love Mick. But since he was as equally unattainable as the Bava Brothers, I was safe in spreading my unrequited love to the masses.

I pined away day after day for the Bava Brothers. Unfortunately, lots of girls loved the Bava Brothers and I was low on the totem pole. Unlike Mick, the Bava Brothers were nice to me, but their hearts went to other girls who didn't have the faint scent of horse and goat.

I used my horse statues to try to psychoanalyze what was going on in my love life. The horses assumed personalities remarkably like my classmates, and I managed to remain relatively sane despite ongoing disappointment and disillusionment with the tastes of the human male.

Autumn was a windy time in the windy city. I pulled on my trusty green plaid wool jacket from Montgomery Ward, stuffed my hands in the pockets, and set out each day for the farm feeling like I was battling a hurricane. The worst was when there was a cold rain with the wind. Dead leaves grew slippery and sodden underfoot, cars along the busy highways splashed me with cold showers of dirty water, and all was grey.

The barn still was scented with fresh hay, and the sweet smell of fresh cow milk from Matilda. With trail rides increasingly cancelled due to weather, there was more time to try to decrease the steady encroachment of manure in the stalls. Mostly, fall was the time to ride the trails during breaks in the weather, or just bring Joe in the barn to brush him, and lean against his growing winter coat.

Mick was increasingly sullen, and strangely quiet. His pranks lost their childish delight, and just grew mean. Whatever was going on with Mick was troubling. The days grew shorter, and darker. And then, my life veered sharply downward along with the temperature.

I went out to the field to get Joe, and noticed him rolling on the ground. It was not the carefree rolls of a horse scratching his back. It was the anguished roll of a horse in pain.

I had never seen anything like it. I crept closer to him, halter in hand, and said in a frightened voice, "Joe? Are you okay?"

He continued writhing on the ground, and then pulled himself up. His lips were stretched back in a grimace. I was terrified. I retreated towards the barn. I needed to get Milly. I ran as fast as I could calling her name.

Joe hung his head, mouth foaming, labored breathing and grunts, watching me. Then, as I neared the barn, he began trotting after me. I turned to see him struggling madly through the mud patch, face contorted, teeth bared.

For the first time in my life, I was afraid of Joe. I wrenched open the barn door. As Joe reached me, his face a mass of pain, I slammed the door on him.

Crying now, I peeked out. Joe stood at the door, sides heaving.

"Milly!!!!" I shrieked.

She came running. We opened the barn door together to see Joe collapsed in the mud, rolling, and groaning in pain. Milly sprang into action. She called to Mick and grabbed my lead rope. I stood at the door, mute and terrified. I had no idea what was happening. Milly looped the rope around Joe's neck while Mick helped shove him from the other side. The two of them managed to get him to his feet.

Joe was still groaning, his face still contorted, lips pulled back. Milly struggled to get the halter on him, finally succeeded, and led him into the barn.

"Colic," she said, to both me and Mick, "I'll call Dr. Milner."

I knew nothing of colic. Milly, seeing my stricken face, handed me the lead.

"Walk him," she said, "Don't stop. Don't let him roll, or lie down. Mick, stay with her. Keep him walking." Mick looked as scared as I was. Neither of us spoke. Joe followed me, at times calmly, and then all of a sudden, as with seized with immense pain, he stumbled, and his front legs started to buckle. Mick smacked at his rump, while I tugged on the lead till he sputtered forward. Keep walking.

Milly, off the phone, joined us now.

"Dr. Milner is on his way. Joe needs to keep walking."

I had no idea why, nor any idea of what was happening, but I trusted Milly, and if she told me Joe must not lie down, then I would not let Joe lie down. She walked with us, she by my side, Mick near Joe's back haunches. We circled the yard as the wind blew and the dead leaves swirled.

"What's colic?" I finally dared to ask.

"It's a blockage in the intestines," said Milly.

"Why do we need to keep walking?"

"If the horse rolls, his intestines can twist and make it worse," she explained, "The most important thing we can do is keep Joe walking and keep him calm till Dr. Milner gets here."

Joe nudged his nose against me, as though pleading with me to take away the pain. I felt terrible that I had run from him when he was only coming to me for comfort. I was his best friend…his only friend…and I had let him down.

"What will Dr. Milner do?"

"He'll examine him and decide if he needs surgery," said Milly, "If we keep walking him, it helps move things along."

"He needs to take a dump," explained Mick. Good old Mick. His irreverence made all of us laugh, though my laughter was a cross between a sob and a chuckle.

"Can I give him a carrot?" I asked.

"No! He can't have anything to eat or drink." She saw me recoil and laid a hand briefly on my arm.

"You are doing just what you need to do. He trusts you and he is staying with you. Just keep walking." She veered away when she saw Dr. Milner's truck pull in. Mick stayed with me and we circled the yard silently, walking poor Joe.

Dr. Milner approached with his doctor bag, stethoscope around his neck. He smiled kindly at me.

"This your horse?" he asked.

I glanced at Milly. "Yes."

"He trusts you. Hold him still now, young lady and let me listen to his belly."

Dr. Milner listened all over Joe's abdomen, while I stroked his nose, and scratched him behind his ears. He leaned his head against me, pushing into me.

"I'm hearing a lot of rumbling," said Dr. Milner, "Let's see what happens if we keep walking a while."

"Vicky," Milly said, "Would you like me to call your mom? Tell her you will be here a while?"

I nodded. The sun was setting, and the night descending. I kept walking. For an hour, with Mick near Joe's rump and me at Joe's head, we silently walked, and walked, and walked.

"Is Joe going to die?" I asked Mick.

"Not if he poops," said Mick.

I prayed and prayed that Joe would poop. I've never wanted manure to materialize as desperately as I wanted it to do so at that moment. Suddenly Joe stopped. I thought he was going to throw himself on the ground again, but instead he lifted his tail, and a huge stream of poop erupted from him.

Mick smiled. "He'll be okay now."

Milly and Dr. Milner cheered. Dr. Milner listened to his gut again. He told Milly Joe should remain in the standing stall that evening but that he was much encouraged.

The doctor patted my shoulder and told me I had been a good little helper. Milly conferred with him as she walked him to his car. I tied Joe in an empty standing stall. Mick let one of the boarder's horses out for the night, so Joe could have the stall. While Milly was talking with Dr. Milner, I brushed Joe.

As I brushed the mud off his neck, I talked to him quietly.

"I love you, Joe, and I'm sorry I ran away. I didn't know you were hurting. You get better and as soon as I get home from school, I will come right over."

Milly returned now and stood near, listening. I glanced up.

"Can we give him some hay?"

"Not tonight," she said, "Dr. Milner says it will be best not to feed him tonight. I'll be back in the morning and feed him then. He'll feel much better by the morning."

I kept brushing him. It was getting late by now, and I had school the next day. I knew I had to go home, but I didn't want to leave.

"I'll drive you home," Milly said, "Mick will watch Joe." Mick stood nearby, having returned from sending the boarder horse out into the dark field. I glanced at him. He nodded.

Hugging Joe, I pressed my cheek against his. I looked into his eyes, peaceful now.

"I'll see you tomorrow, Joe. Good boy."

If I could have spent the night there, I would have. But I couldn't. I pet his neck, kissed his muzzle, and followed Milly out to her car.

"He'll be okay," she promised, as she dropped me at my house.

Chapter Twenty Four

Agony stabbed me like knives, as I sat through school the next day. All I could think about was Joe. Even Mark and Mike Bava failed to get me to smile. I couldn't answer a single question in class, causing my teacher to ask me if I had left my thinking cap at home. She didn't say it in a mean way. She looked worried.

I didn't want to talk about it. I knew Joe was going to be okay, but my spirit felt dead inside me. I know that is strange, but that's how I felt. I was terribly worried, and knew I wouldn't feel better till I was holding Joe's soft muzzle against my cheek.

When the bell rang, and school was out I dashed to the bus. Sometimes we had to wait when our bus driver was late, but for once, she was on time. I sat near the front so I could be the first one out. I hardly noticed the bully teasing the kid behind me. Usually I felt like I might explode over the meanness, but all I thought about was how many minutes it would take me to get home and change into my farm clothes.

Mom abandoned Benign Neglect for an afternoon. She told me she had a special little bag of greens and carrots for Joe all ready for me. I grabbed the baggie of goodies after setting a world record for getting out of my school clothes and into my barn clothes. Then I dashed out the door and ran as fast as I could all the way to the farm.

As I careened around the corner, Zeke barked like the maniac he was, and the stallion continued his quest to kick his shed to smithereens. I barely registered anything. I did notice Milly and Mick standing at the barn door, looking out, as though they were waiting for me.

Then I noticed their faces, and I stopped running.

"Vicky," Milly said softly, "Joe didn't make it."

Mick looked at me with what I can only describe as sorrow though that is, of course, impossible, knowing Mick.

"He didn't make *what*?" I asked, not understanding.

"He died. His intestines were just too twisted."

I gaped at her, incredulous.

"That's impossible…he was better."

"He did seem better, but he wasn't. He was in terrible pain. The vet had to put him down early this morning."

And I wasn't there to say Goodbye.

Without a word, I ran. I ran through the yard, and climbed the fence, jumping into the pasture. I don't know why I was running or where I was running to. I guess I thought if I ran fast enough, I could outrun the grief.

I was wrong.

I ran to the end of the pasture, and then doubled over, out of breath. I still had the baggie of special treats in my hand. When I noticed

Vicky Kaseorg

that, I burst into tears. Clutching the baggie, I walked slowly back along the fence to the little pond by the crab-apple tree where Joe loved to stand in the shade.

Then I sat at the base of the tree, and buried my head in my arms. I was surprised it was possible to cry so hard without   crumbling into little pieces as the cells dried up. There could not have been an ounce of tears left in me after the first hour or so. Then I glanced at the special treat in the baggie. Wrong again. It was like Noah's flood. Forty days and forty nights could not have produced the deluge pouring out of me.

I kept remembering the first time I saw Joe, the ugly horse no one loved. He was so dejected, head hanging low, all by himself. I remembered brushing him, and how he liked to nibble on my shirt looking for carrots. I remembered how long it took for him to let the saddle near, but then how he trusted me so much, he didn't act like it was the slightest big deal to put it on him. I remembered the first time driving him in the little cart – how proud he was, and how his tail streamed behind him. I remembered barrel racing, and how I was just along for the ride, hanging on for dear life. I remembered baby Holly on his back, and how gentle he was. I remembered snuggling against his shaggy coat on cold winter days. I didn't know God then, except for the God of my keychain, but if God was there, why would He take the one thing this lonely little girl had loved so much?

That thought provoked a whole new onslaught of wailing sobs. My shirt was covered in tears and snot. Heart-felt grief is messy. I don't know how long I sat there sobbing at the end of my world, but it was a long time. I finally just couldn't breathe because all my air passages were swollen shut. I had to stop crying or asphyxiate. Little gulps of grief bubbled out. I didn't move my head, still buried against my knees in my arms, when I heard steps approaching.

I knew Milly would come eventually, but how I wished she wouldn't. Words would not fix this. Nothing would fix this. This was one of those things, as my keychain foretold, *I cannot change.*

"Vicky?" a deep voice spoke tentatively into my darkness.

Mick?? I turned my head just enough to crack open one eye. What was Mick doing here? Surely he wasn't so cruel as to gloat now, in my hour of deepest despair. I felt fury begin to replace the grief.

And then, a hand gently fell on my shoulder.

"I'm really sorry, Vicky. I know how much you loved Joe."

I thought there could be no more tears, but I was wrong (again.) Mick's tenderness made me even sadder than before for some reason. It was as if all the hurt for all the things I could not control came gushing out of me. A regular Niagara Falls of sorrow.

"And he loved you. Joe didn't love *anyone*…but he did love you."

Mick sat beside me, patting my shoulder while I cried and cried and cried. You might think I am being redundant here but if I added twenty more "cried" to the list, it would not be sufficient. Milly must have given him special permission, because night was falling and someone else must have been doing the chores.

Finally, I sputtered to a stop.

"You could pick a new horse," Mick offered.

"I don't want another horse!" I wailed, and the endless river reached flood stage again.

"But what if there was another horse that needed you? Like Joe needed you?"

I glanced up with my incredibly attractive green-snotted cheeks, red rimmed eyes, and swollen eyelids. He was crafty, I will give him that. I was instantly wondering what horse he meant.

"Like who?"

"Witch. No one can ride Witch. Everybody hates Witch. Witch has nothing worth-while in any part of her ugly body. Isn't that the sort of horse you go for?"

I stopped crying. It's true. I had wondered what the farm was going to do about Witch, but was so consumed with Joe that I didn't give her much thought. Not even Mick ever tried to ride her.

Mick watched me as I rubbed my goopy nose on my sodden sleeve. I gazed across the pasture. Witch stood slightly apart from the other horses, her slender young form in sharp contrast to the old nags nearby.

"Her name's not Witch," I said, standing up.

Mick looked at me with forehead furrowed. He probably thought my brains had leaked out with all the tears.

"Yes it is…"

"No," I said firmly, "If she's my horse, then her name is Gidget."

Then I headed down the field as the sun threw its last amber rays heavenward. Mick watched me walk towards the dappled grey Gidget, shaking his head. For once, he was the one left speechless.

Vicky on Gidget – 1970

Background colored by author, age 13, of a yellow brick road

Afterword

I knew Joe fifty years ago. His death was the first serious heartbreak of my life. Writing this story was effortless. It flowed out of me, sometimes ten-thousand words a day.

Then I reached the last chapter. I wrote it while sobbing as hard as I did when I was a little girl facing the death of my beloved horse. Since I was freaking out my dogs, I locked myself in the bathroom. Fortunately, the rest of my family was out. I cried and cried thinking how little I like being unable to control pain, suffering, and death. I didn't like it fifty years ago and I don't like it now.

The wool jacket I used to wear to the farm still hangs in my closet, though it smells a whole lot better. Since I hit full size around age twelve and stayed approximately the same weight and size my whole life, it still fits. The jacket means a lot to me.

One family of horse statues still reside with me. All the others have been lost in the graveyard of time. I am not sure what I did with them. But

I kept my little horse stallion, mare, and foal, loving the unity and love of that little family. It was how it seemed the world should be.

My keychain, Goldie still lives in her little silver box in a dresser drawer. I have a terrible memory, but from the time I found Goldie when I was eight-years-old, I memorized the serenity prayer and have never forgotten it. It is a wise prayer, but a difficult one.

In hind sight, I realize now that if Joe hadn't died, I don't know how I could have ever left Chazak. When my Dad got a new job in NY shortly after Joe's death, we had to move. It was hard enough leaving Burton's Farm. It would have been impossible leaving Joe. He had to leave me first.

I never again connected to a horse the way I did to Joe. I rode quite a bit as I grew up, but never found another farm to work on, and we couldn't afford a horse. When I did have the opportunity to ride, even decades later, the horses' owners always mentioned that I was an unusual trail rider. I had "soft hands."

For fifty years, I wanted to tell the story of Joe, and I am glad that I finally have.

As I wrote the last chapter of Joe, I thought of how I have never had an easy time accepting the things I cannot change. God may have seemed cruel to me then, but not anymore. Now that I know Him better, I realize Joe was mine for a season when I most needed him. I was being prepared for the seasons of when others would need me. Perhaps more importantly, I understood who *was* in control of all things, and that trusting Him even in my deepest, darkest pain was necessary. I had to lose what I clung to most tightly in order to gain what I could never lose.

I know horses are in heaven. How comforting are those Bible verses about "chariots of fire" in the sky! I look forward to seeing Joe again. If anyone deserves a chariot of fire, it is Joe. Imagine me and Joe, as the clouds of glory sift through our hair, taking a victory lap with him in the heavenly harness!

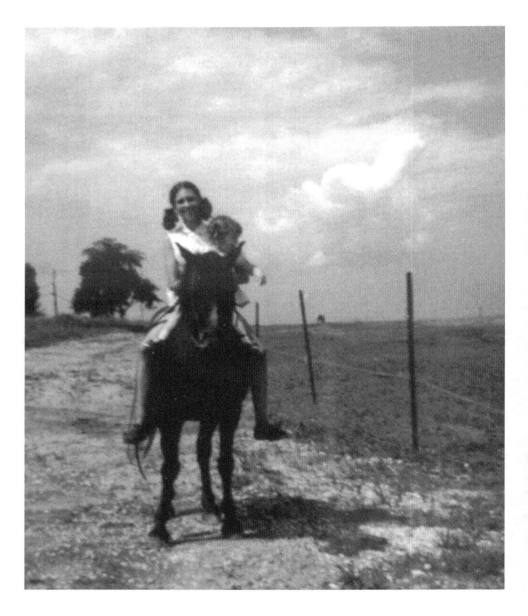

Other Books by Vicky Kaseorg

I'm Listening with a Broken Ear- 2011

God Drives a Tow Truck- 2011

Tommy- a Story of Ability- 2012

Turning Points-The Life of a Milne Bay WWII Gunner- 2012

The Illustrated 23rd Psalm- 2012

The Good Parent- 2012

The Well-Trained Human- 2012

Saving a Dog- 2014

The Tower Builder – 2014

The Bark of the Covenant – 2014

Poppy- The Dirty Ditch Digging Dingo – 2015

The Paws That Bring Good News – 2015

What the Reviewers Are Saying

Listening with a Broken Ear:

*This book is simply amazing, one of the best non-fiction books I've read in a very long time.

*This is a wonderful book. The author has a remarkable sense of humor and had me laughing out loud at her remarks

God Drives a Tow Truck:

*The precision, depth, tone and tenor in her writing is exquisite

*I wish I could give this book 6 stars. It is a delight. Inspiring, heart warming mmm mmm good. A must read

*I love this book! It is so awesome and inspiring! These stories touched my core and made me want to deepen my faith more. I hope the author writes another one.

Tommy- A Story of Ability:

*A simple story of acceptance of who (or what) you are, rising above your circumstance to let yourself be happy, and (if you read between the lines) knowing that God simply don't make no junk. Not since Stein's dog Enzo wrote "The Art of Racing in the Rain" has another doggy author touched the heart strings with their philosophical approach to life.

* quote an old song title, Tommy had the right idea - accentuate the positive and eliminate the negative. And he doesn't seem to mess with Mr. In-Between either. So by now I guess you can tell that I'm not one of your younger readers but that certainly didn't keep me from enjoying this well-written, upbeat little book on a day when I really needed something positive to focus on.

*What a wonderful book! I loved every minute of it. She writes beautifully and anyone that is an animal lover (or even an animal "liker") will love this book. She has a way with words that leave all of us feeling better when we've read the book.

I highly recommend this book - and any other she has written!

Poppy- the Dirty Ditch Digging Dingo

*...It is a tour-de-force triumph, and a book I've never before in all my 85 years experienced. We loved it . . . and so will you!

*It took about 20 minutes to read this heart-warming story about Poppy and her inspiring determination in life! She knows her strengths and her need to dig symbolizes her knowledge of her purpose. We all need purpose in our lives and something to look forward to each day.

*Wish I could give this book 10 stars! AWESOME book!!!! Adult or child everyone will enjoy it. I HIGHLY recommend this endearing tale of Poppy and her human.

The Bark of the Covenant

5.0 out of 5 stars Perfect! Just Perfect! August 14, 2014
Vicky Kaseorg's The Bark of the Covenant deserves a perfect 5-star rating. The characters resonate so strongly with readers that they would be recognized if they knocked on the front door. Carolina Dogs (North American Dingoes also called "yaller dogs" and "swamp dogs") are an integral part of the story, believably and brilliantly moving the plot as they pique readers' curiosity about America's ancient wild dog breed.

The Paws That Bring Good News

5.0 out of 5 stars

The characters' stories are beautifully woventogether in a small southern town March 7, 2015

I couldn't put this book down. The characters' stories are beautifully woven together in a small southern town. The plot combines so many elements that are dear to me: Carolina Dogs, the goodness of God, humor, gentle hints of romance, mystery, and major questions in life. The author writes about sensitive issues with such compassion, such as making decisions about abortion and adoption. I just finished it, but I think I will have to read it again because I'm attached to the characters and not ready to let them go! I hope there will be more Whipporwill Chronicles!

The Tower Builder

5.0 out of 5 stars A well told story of Love and passion in several shades...none of them grey but all inspired., March 7, 2015

This review is from: The Tower Builder: Love story, history, WWII mystery, and biography intersect in this true story of the most dangerous job in the world. (Kindle Edition)

People assume that Engineers are dispassionate...dealing in facts, making purely logical decisions, putting aside emotion...so totally wrong...this book captures the true spirit of two Engineers brought together to restore a legendary Broadcast facility after hurricane Hugo. In coming to know them the author made a fascinating journey through the history of Radio Broadcasting in the U.S. Mysteries are solved...secrets of government-broadcaster cooperation are revealed...the emotional intelligence of truly passionate Engineers is realized...all in a wonderfully entertaining read.

*****

Please visit my facebook page and "like" it for regular updates on new books/writing. I love to hear from readers!

https://www.facebook.com/pages/Vicky-Kaseorg-Author/344952178879131

Twitter: https://twitter.com/vickykaseorg

Follow me on my daily inspirational blog at vicky.kaseorg@blogspot.com

Stay abreast of new publications at my author page at: http://www.amazon.com/Vicky-Kaseorg/e/B006XJ2DWU

If you enjoyed this book, please go to Amazon, or wherever you purchased this book, and write a review! Much appreciated!

Vicky Kaseorg

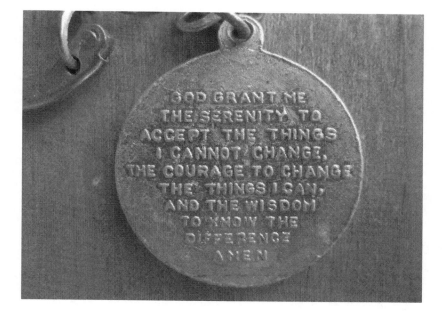

Vicky Kaseorg

Coming Soon- Sequel

Gidget – the Horse Formerly Known As Witch

Chapter One

Ok, if you read my first story about my horse Joe, Gidget's predecessor, you probably finished crying a few tubs-full of tears after a year or so. Don't worry. Gidget's story isn't nearly as bittersweet. It *is* just as good, but in a different way. All encounters with animals that seemingly have no value seem to teach me about the intrinsic value of life. Gidget had just as important a message for me as my first horse did. I cannot guarantee there will be no tears, but you don't need to buy stock in Kleenex to get through the story of Gidget.

My initial attempts at telling her the exciting news that she would be my new horse didn't go nearly as well as I expected. Joe had just died, and I *wanted* to. That's where the last book left off and this book begins. I didn't think I would survive, particularly since I knew from my science class that 75% of the human being is water. Since I had cried at least that much, only 25% of me remained. That is *for sure* how I felt. But then the strangest thing happened. Mick, the boy I'd swooned over for three desperate, unrequited years took a sudden turn into nice-ville. For three years, he had called me every name in the book, and treated me like the scum I knew deep in my heart I was. Until Joe died. When Joe died, for one brief shining moment, Mick acted like he had a heart. My own heart was completely broken by the death of Joe and I barely registered Mick's moment of civility. Instead, I dried my tears and the 25% of me that was left sought comfort through the only horse that needed me as much as Joe had on Burton's Farm.

You would think some 6th sense that animals have would have alerted the flighty, grey-speckled horse to approach me in my hour of need. Didn't she feel the despair leaking out of me like I'd been shot a thousand times? Aren't animals supposed to cue in to those vibes? And if she couldn't sense my grief, you would think she would at least have smelled the baggie of sumptuous goodies Mom had prepared for Joe, not knowing Joe would never munch anything this side of heaven again. Instead, the dapple-grey ignored my tear-stained cheeks, my angst which was shouting loud and clear to anyone paying attention, *and* my baggie of lettuce and carrots. She glanced at me, and then galloped away.

I stood watching her disappear over the dip in the field. I would probably have started crying again, but one of the nice horses, Beauty, had snuck up on me and snatched my baggie of goodies. And then she started trotting off after Gidget. I have to admit, at that point I was ready to restore Gidget to her original name, Witch, but didn't have the emotional energy to be vindictive. I had only chosen the name Gidget five minutes earlier when on a moment of impulse decided the skittery, crazy Witch was the horse I would shower my love upon. It was my vote of confidence for the loco horse, my benediction, my prophesy of her great future. I guess I expected instant gratitude. But if she was grateful, the horse formerly known as Witch preferred to express her thanks as far away from me as possible.

Why *Gidget*? Believe it or not, there was a logical reason for choosing that name if one, like me, is the queen of loose association. *The Flying Nun* was a popular show back then, in the late 60s. I loved Sally Fields, the star of *The Flying Nun*, and that is when she produced her one music album with the song that had been running through my head when Joe died. It was called *Things Look Their Darkest Right Before Dawn.*

I especially had loved Sally Fields in the role of Gidget, the show she did before *The Flying Nun*. So as I was walking towards the skittery horse, trying to catch her while dabbing at tears, I was remembering that song: *Things Look Their Darkest Right Before Dawn.* Sally Fields made me think of Gidget, and voila, Witch had a new name.

But she didn't seem eager to claim it. As I darted after Beauty and my goodie bag dangling from her teeth, I noticed Gidget (Witch) in the distance, still galloping over the next rise and fall of the field. Good grief. You'd think I was a pack of wolves rather than a mournful twelve-year-old girl who had just endured the most tragic moment of my life.

Like I said, my horse Joe had just died. The love of my life, my only friend, the sad little horse that I had rehabilitated with nothing but love in my arsenal of expertise for the past three years since my family moved to Chazak, Illinois. I would have gone into months of mourning, but then Mick, who had never said a kind thing to me, snuck up on me sobbing in the pasture and reminded me about Gidget. He told me Gidget needed me, and I realized he was right.

No one liked Gidget, just as no one had liked Joe. Other than that, they were not at all alike. Joe was old, small, sway-backed, and dark with a well-rounded droopy belly. Gidget was tall, thin, and young, a light dappled grey, quick and light on her feet. Joe hated everyone. Well, everyone but me. Gidget *feared* everyone. Including me. Even with my strong enticement of a goodie bag with lettuce and carrots. Gidget refused to go near anyone, unless tricked and grabbed quickly before she skittered away. I don't think she was mean, but she certainly wasn't trusting of humans.

Meanwhile, Beauty was still trotting just out of reach and gradually consuming the plastic bag along with its contents. How she managed to slowly draw the plastic bag into her mouth while running from me was almost magical. Still, I knew that consuming plastic which takes

10,000 years to decay in landfills could not be the best thing in the world for her, but my little legs had no hope of catching her. I kept running, giving it my best shot. No good. When she had gobbled down the last morsel of plastic, she stopped and looked kindly back at me. I huffed and puffed up to her, and fell against her side. She swallowed with a gulp, and twitched her tail. We both looked to the horizon, where Gidget was still galloping, leaving a trail of dust in her wake. I figured by the time she hit the fence, she would put on the brakes. Nope. She just slowed to a canter and continued along the fence till a copse of trees blotted her from my view.

Sighing, I headed back to the barn. Milly, the wife of Burton and co-owner of Burton's Farm, was (as usual) busy with chores. Her long braid lay down the center of her back, with a few wisps of hair loosened and drifting about her sun-dried face. She and Mick, her son and permanent miscreant, were both tossing flakes of hay to the barn horses. Mick glanced at me, and looked uncomfortable. I knew exactly what he was thinking. Since he had been nice to me for a full twenty seconds or so while I was gushing tears in the pasture over poor old Joe, he probably thought I expected him to continue behaving that way. Believe me, I had no such delusions. I was still the tongue-tied "hay-head" he hated, and had despised from the moment he met me three years ago. Milly, however, paused in her work and came to me. Her weathered face, covered in fissures and cracks like a crumpled piece of cellophane was kindly, filled with sympathy. It was she who an hour or so ago had broken the news to me that Joe had died. I reacted with what they call in Biology the "fright or flight" syndrome. I chose to flee from that awful news as fast as I could into the pasture. It was probably Milly's idea to send Mick to comfort me. Now, she likely felt she had to offer her condolences, much as I would rather pretend Joe had never existed than have to suffer his loss or anyone's pity. For one frightful moment, I thought she might hug me. I loved Milly, but I didn't like anyone touching me. She fortunately reconsidered, and just laid a hand on my shoulder.

"I'm sorry about Joe."

I felt fresh tears starting up. Mick must have seen them too, because he dashed away with armfuls of hay, a worried look on his face.

"Mick says you talked about wanting Witch to be your horse."

I wiped at the tears, and nodded.

"I don't know if she's interested," I said. I considered telling her Beauty had eaten a plastic bag, but instead remained silent, hoping Beauty's clogged intestines would not be on my conscience.

"Well, frankly it would not be a good idea," Milly said. I blinked, wondering *what* would not be a good idea. I'd been sidetracked by considering Beauty's potential demise from the baggie of goodies. Oh yeah. Gidget/Witch.

"That's what you said about Joe," I reminded her.

"That's true. And what you did with Joe surprised me. But Witch is a whole different matter. Joe was mean, but at least he was predictable. What makes Witch dangerous is she is so unpredictable. One moment she is quietly standing with her eyes closed, and the next moment, she's knocking down a fence to get away. It's like she's possessed. That's why we call her Witch."

"I want to call her Gidget."

"Mick mentioned that. I wish changing a horse's name was all it took to change her behavior."

I noticed Mick tiptoeing back into the main room of the barn, eyeing me as he snatched another armful of hay and raced off down another hallway lined with stalls. Maybe he was turning over a new leaf in our relationship. He had gone at least fifteen minutes in my presence without a single nasty jab tossed my way like a grenade.

Milly gazed at me, still resting her hand on my shoulder. She was not a touchy feely type, and I sure wasn't. I was wishing she would remove her hand but it seemed rude to mention that, so I just nodded. That was always my "go to" communication mode when words failed me. Which happened *always*.

"I think it would not be wise to have you work with Witch."

"Gidget."

"OK, Gidget. I think it is possible she would kill you. Not on purpose, but she needs an experienced trainer. She is barely green-broke, and needs someone who has dealt with her issues before."

I didn't speak. Part of me knew Milly was right. The other part of me was crumbling in a billion pieces of sadness over Joe. It was crazy to think I could help Gidget, but if I didn't, who would?

"Not that any of us could…" Milly said, echoing my own thoughts.

"So what will you do with her?"

"Sell her, if we can find someone crazy enough to buy her," Milly answered.

"You'd get more money if she could be safely ridden."

Milly cocked her head and took her hand off my shoulder (Thank God!), putting both hands on her hips.

"You have a point."

Made in the USA
Middletown, DE
27 October 2016